FINDING MARJORIE KING

A daughter's journey to discover her mother's identity

JENNIFER DURRANT & CHERYL ROGERS

First published 2022

Big Sky Publishing Pty Ltd
PO Box 303, Newport, NSW 2106, Australia
Phone: 1300 364 611
Fax: (61 2) 9918 2396
Email: info@bigskypublishing.com.au
Web: www.bigskypublishing.com.au

Cover design and typesetting: Think Productions

A catalogue record for this book is available from the National Library of Australia

FINDING MARJORIE KING

A daughter's journey to discover her mother's identity

www.bigskypublishing.com.au

JENNIFER DURRANT & CHERYL ROGERS

Dedicated to all descendants of
Marjorie D'Antoine King York (1924–2007),
so they may know her story. May it inspire
others to never, never give up on a quest.

CONTENTS

First Nations people are advised that this book contains depictions and names of deceased Aboriginal and Torres Strait Islander people, and content that may be considered culturally sensitive.

PROLOGUE

Sixty years ago, in the beautiful Swan Valley, outside Perth in Western Australia, a little girl called Jennifer used to look at a portrait and wonder. The photo was of her mother, a softly spoken, gentle woman, who never spoke about her past.

'Where is Mum's family? Who are they? Why are they never talked about? Why are there no photographs of Mum until she met Dad? Where are the photographs of Mum as a child?' These were among the myriad questions swimming through Jennifer's mind. She needed answers. Marjorie's family was Jennifer's family, too.

The silence from her mother's past was made all the more obvious by the noise and conviviality surrounding her father's family. A steady stream of visitors including uncles, aunts, in-laws and cousins would come and go from their West Swan farm, sharing Marjorie's hospitality and conversation. Jennifer would overhear those conversations. They made no mention of Marjorie's early life before she had met and married the love of her life, the man who became Jennifer's father.

As Jennifer grew older, her curiosity only deepened about this real-life mystery at the centre of her own identity. Whenever she questioned Marjorie, the answers would always be brief and unwilling, often through tears. The names of key players were recorded as Doris

Schulze, Quan Sing, Una F. Ulrich, Rosalie and Mabel Ross Sharp. Who were they? At what point had they intersected the timeline of Marjorie's life?

Along the way, Jennifer's childhood school friend Cheryl found herself pulled into the mystery. Cheryl was an experienced researcher and writer with a special interest in genealogy. She estimated that cracking the Marjorie King case would take, maybe, six months. False leads and even misinformation conspired to spin that deadline way, way out of control.

Then a serendipitous connection happened. It involved a wedding, two christenings, and another wedding, 20 years after the first.

The search gained momentum as more and more people jumped aboard, captivated by the intrigue and keen to help Jennifer discover the answers she so desperately needed. Like all mysteries, the road to resolution described here contains elements of suspense, a few red herrings, some fiercely strong characters and scientific evidence.

There is also a remarkable twist, which confirms the power of communication and connection and the undying strength of family love. Jennifer's journey of discovery occupied over a half century of her life.

On this ultimately triumphant journey, which is emotional but often frustrating, we learn the secrets of the characters and discover how completely a person can disappear with the stroke of a pen.

PART ONE

JENNIFER'S MUM

Jennifer Durrant

– JD –

Cheryl Rogers

– CR –

1

THE LIGHTNING BOLT

– JD –

I was about six years old when a bolt of lightning shot through our kitchen louvres and blew the arse out of the fridge. It's lucky it wasn't meal time, because I was sitting where my brother Philip always sat when our family gathered around the laminex table for breakfast, lunch and dinner. Eight-and-a-half years older than me, Philip was also quite a bit taller and broader. The streak of electricity entered through the open louvres on the northwest corner of that room, shot just over my left shoulder and took out the button in the middle of the fridge door behind me.

Afterwards, I was aware of the smell of burning, the blackened fridge door handle and the knowledge that Mum and Dad would have to fork out for a new fridge. That would cost them, but our round-shouldered cream Kelvinator was a goner. I think the gods must have been moving that day. Had Philip been sitting where I was, he wouldn't have stood a chance. And had I been a little older, just a bit taller, I might not be telling you this story today. As it was, we all just happened to be in the right place at the right time. The members of our family, that is, not the fridge.

I am the youngest of Marjorie and Henry York's four children. Our home back then was a five-room asbestos cottage with a tin roof, on 10 acres in West Swan in the beautiful Swan Valley, near Perth. Ours was a small farm in the bush and backed on to the old Caversham Airfield, which in those days was a motor-racing circuit, all happening just over our back fence. It was around the time of the lightning strike that the famous Jack Brabham, later Sir Jack Brabham AM, OBE, raced there.

We'd run a little sideline on race days, allowing race fans to park on our place for a fee. And after it was all over, we'd climb through the post-and-wire fence to the racetrack and collect as many discarded empty drink bottles as we could carry. Dad would cart them all off to a marine dealer and let us share the earnings. That was our pocket money. Mum even had a few driving lessons out on that airstrip with Dad trying to teach her. It was where most of the locals went to learn to drive. Not that Mum had much success – she didn't get her licence until years later, after I'd finished school. I guess it was always going to be hard trying to concentrate, with four young children packed into the back seat. Apparently, I was an angel. It was the others who mucked around and put her off.

Dad was very mindful of managing our land properly, keeping a healthy balance, having worked on a lot of farms like his father before him. Our bush was full of wildflowers – kangaroo paws, smokey bush, orchids – and in the paddocks and pens we ran sheep, chooks and geese. There was usually a goose baking in the wood oven at Christmas, so you can imagine how hot it got in that kitchen. Even years later, when we got a small electric oven, which sat on the benchtop, the wood stove was still used.

The garden beds around our house grew just about everything it was possible to grow including silverbeet, cabbage, cauliflowers, peas, beans, corn, onions and rhubarb. All sorts of fruit trees, including an enormous mulberry tree. The house still stands today where for the past century it has looked out across the front paddock towards Edward Street, set back a little from the main road.

Back then, in the early Sixties, we all had our set place around the table and were expected to stick to it. It was probably my parents' way of maintaining some sort of order amidst the occasional chaos of family life. Dad sat at the head of the table at the south end, where he had a good view of both the back and front doors and could also keep an eye on all of us. Philip sat to his right next to my other brother George, with my sister Dawn at the north end near the wood stove, facing Dad. I sat to Dad's immediate left, with Mum immediately to my left – so I the youngest was firmly planted between both parents. Despite this structure, we were encouraged to join in lively discussions around the table. It was not a matter of children being seen and not heard, not in our house.

Dad believed it was important to know as much as possible about a subject, because that way we were less likely to come to grief, by experimenting to find out, for ourselves. Take sex, for instance. It was discussed along with politics, no topic was taboo. However, I seem to recall that when I was very small, there were times when I would be asked to leave the room for a few minutes, until the talk around the table had cooled down a bit.

From this young age, I was also aware that both my parents were very capable people.

Mum even used some home remedies to treat our cuts and scratches, like the time I stood on a broken lupin stalk. She made a poultice out of soap, sugar, bread and onion and applied it, to draw out the poison overnight. The same remedy was used to treat an infected cat scratch on my arm that was bubbling with pus.

Dad had virtually rebuilt our house, which had belonged to his parents. My grandfather George William York had died in 1943, when Dad was just 22, but Dad's mother Eliza often stayed with us. Apparently, she was very tall and thin and had towered over my grandfather who was relatively short. She had white, white hair and used to let us roll her cigarettes.

As our family grew, Dad added a sleep-out to the south end as a main bedroom for him and Mum. It had a big bank of louvre windows along the length of the south wall. The boys occupied the bedroom opposite the kitchen, while Dawn and I slept in the girls' room adjacent to the kitchen and opposite the family lounge.

Outside, Dad built the bathroom in a separate annex just off the kitchen. Every morning and night, he'd light the chip-wood heater to warm the water for our morning and night-time baths – yes, we bathed twice each day. It was a family ritual. Whoever happened to be the cleanest went first. This was before we became old enough to take on the responsibility of lighting the wood heater ourselves.

Right next to the bathroom, he built a huge pantry which Mum managed to fill because she was always pickling and bottling. She had a Fowlers Vacola kit and kept the shelves full of jars of pickled onions, bottled apples, pears, you name it, she even pickled fish.

In the gap between the pantry and the kitchen, Dad built us a proper, undercover toilet. It saved us shooting up the back to the outhouse in the bush beyond the house at all hours. This was around the time that the dunny man with the night cart stopped calling at our place.

Money was tight and for Mum and Dad that meant saving as much as they could by using what they grew. Bartering was also the norm. We would often trade surplus vegetables with nearby families in return for a few grapes or melons, when they had an oversupply. Dad also grew mushrooms and supplied the Perth market with Cape gooseberries, which were packed inside thin ply punnets.

He built all our cupboards in that green and white kitchen, even installing a big block of marble on one of the benchtops for Mum to make pastry. She was a wonderful cook, her sausage rolls were amazing.

We always had a full, cooked breakfast before leaving for work or school. This usually started with porridge or some other oat-based cereal followed by scrambled, fried or boiled eggs with toast soldiers. Or smoked fish.

At 6.45am, just as the ABC news was starting on the wireless, Dad would pick up his brown Gladstone bag and head off to drive to the Midland Railway workshops. Before the workshops, he'd been a farm labourer working mainly around local vineyards including several years with prominent table grape pioneer Phil Taylor in West Swan. At the workshops he worked as a moulder's assistant.

He'd also served in the Australian Army in World War II and not long afterwards he met Marjorie, who was working as a nurse's aide at the Mount Hospital in Perth.

Apparently, Dad was a very good dancer unlike Mum, so they both said. Not that I thought too deeply about this back then, because there was not really much time for dancing. We were all too busy growing food, getting an education, working, surviving.

In their sleep-out bedroom, Mum had an old treadle Singer sewing machine and with it she made all our clothes. Everything from undies and pyjamas to dresses, shorts and shirts. She always kept a big stock of materials, all different colours and textures and heaps of wool.

Once, when she caught me looking at one of her wedding photographs that stood on the dresser in their bedroom, she told me that she had made her own wedding dress. The bodice was an intricate latticework, all handmade. I remember being really impressed – not that it has ever inspired me to pick up a needle and cotton – but even then, I could appreciate the skill that was needed to create something so beautiful. I was pretty impressed by the photograph of Mum as a bride. She was absolutely beautiful. Even more stunning than her exquisite dress. Another photograph showed her arriving at the church on the arm of an older man, who I did not recognise.

'Who is he?' I asked.

'Just a friend,' was all she said.

Afterwards, whenever I asked that question, I always got the same answer. So much for the open family discussions around our kitchen table. I sensed quite early that, for Mum at least there were some subjects she just was not comfortable to share.

I stopped asking about the mystery gentleman, a tall man with strong facial features in a pin-striped suit, and managed to convince myself that it was probably her friend Betty Lund's father. Betty and Mum had remained friends since their working days at the Mount Hospital. He would be a logical choice to give Mum away, wouldn't he? But, when my thoughts moved on later, the question in my mind was always, 'Where was Mum's father?'

Next door in the lounge room, another portrait of Mum stood on the sideboard. This was a coloured image of a slightly younger

Marjorie. She's wearing a green dress, with some pleated detail across the shoulders and bodice, set against a peach background. Her dark hair is rolled back and framing her face.

I still think as I always have that she is absolutely gorgeous. And it is so Mum. What I can so clearly see now is that she looks so Asian.

Back then, as a child, I didn't see her as Asian at all. I just saw her as the woman who was my mother. Mum was Mum.

It was around this time, however, that I also started to become aware that Mum didn't talk about her family. It was not that she didn't talk about them much, she didn't talk about them at all. Full stop.

The contrast with Dad's side of the family was becoming increasingly obvious to me. Dad was from a huge York family. His parents had 12 children, 10 of whom had survived childhood. Dad himself was a twin to his brother Lance, our uncle.

So, I was used to a steady stream of York uncles, aunts and cousins, coming and going up the track that led from West Swan Road to our house.

They'd usually park near the huge mulberry tree outside the garage. It was home to our white corella Yogi, a bird that absolutely adored Dawn. And utterly loathed me.

Another car from back then was a flash, big, dark grey sedan. Inside were two quite tiny, older women who would visit specifically to see Mum. They must have called in on more than one occasion, because they are firmly planted in my memory.

Because I am three years younger than my next-eldest sibling George, I had time at home alone with Mum when the others were off at school. Maybe, that gave me the chance to observe events and circumstances that I could not hope to process, until much, much later.

Back then, a woman without a car had to rely on others to get around or use the West Swan bus service, which was pretty limited. So, on payday, which was Thursday every fortnight, Dad would drive home at lunchtime to pick up Mum and take her back to Midland to do a big shop. Mum had a shopping trolley on wheels which would go into the back of the station wagon. Dad would park the car in a location central to the places Mum would visit – the supermarket, butcher, bank and post office – and he'd leave her shopping, while he walked back to work for the afternoon.

One of our occasional visitors was Dad's brother and sister-in-law, Uncle Fred and Auntie Gwen. They lived in Dalwallinu, a small country town in the Western Australian wheat belt and must have made an early start on those two and a half-hour drives to our place, because they usually called in around breakfast time.

On one of their visits, I was sitting with Auntie Gwen warming ourselves by the wood stove. I don't remember any of the others being there, not even Mum. This would have been when I was between the age of about six and 13, the primary school years.

Auntie Gwen was talking to me and told me I needed to talk to Doris Schulze, a woman she knew from Dalwallinu. Maybe I'd said something to her about wanting to know more about Mum's family. I didn't know how to spell Schulze and I don't know why Auntie Gwen singled me out to mention her. What she said didn't make much sense to me, but I never forgot that name.

It would be years, in fact decades, before I would discover the significance of Doris Schulze. She would prove to be another piece of the scattered jigsaw that I would eventually start to put together.

Our mailbox was down at the road. It was made of tin and it was huge. It had to be because it not only took the mail, but also the bread that was delivered each day by the man we called Jim the Baker. If we were hungry, the York kids could get through a half loaf of bread on the way from the mailbox to the house, but we copped it when we got back home the few times that happened.

In spring, when Royal Show time was getting closer, we'd set up a stall on the side of the road near the mailbox selling kangaroo paws and smokey bush from our property, as well as homegrown gooseberries and mulberries. Mum and Dad let us spend whatever we made at the Royal Show, so there was some incentive to make a go of it.

We always looked forward to our trips to the beach. Every summer, Dad would take a month's leave from the workshops and take us to the beach every second day. I think Mum was the driving force, she loved the beach and was never happier than when she had a line in her hands, fishing.

We used to head out to the area, near what is now Burns Beach, and take off through the sandhills in the family station wagon. It didn't matter if we got bogged, there were plenty of hands available to rock us out of the sand.

I loved the beach as a child and still swim most days, through the warmer weather. One of my habits as a kid was to roll over and over, through the beach sand, until I looked like I'd been coated in sugar.

Without fail, Mum was always the last one out of the water when it came time to head home. There were often times when Dad had packed up the car and us and we were all ready to go and Mum would still be in the water. Dad would be calling her, but she was determined to cast out, just one more time, you couldn't stop her.

One time, Dad had to race into the water at the last minute, to help Mum bring in a shark that had bitten off the hook. My friend Cheryl was with us that time. It caused a bit of excitement seeing

Mum in the water like that, with a shark on the loose. Another time, Mum caught three sharks and sold them to one of the local fish and chip shops. Fishing was one of those times when Mum seemed to be as happy as we ever saw her. There were prawning trips to South Perth and other fishing trips to Moore River to catch cobbler and kangaroo ticks.

Mum had big, silver-white scars, above and below her left knee, from where she was attacked by a shark when she was fishing when she was young. This must have been in Carnarvon, the coastal town, 900 km north of Perth, where she told me she'd spent her childhood. The shark bite apparently happened when she was about 15 years old. The scars were white and raised, so it must have been quite a decent-sized shark. It marked her for life.

Sometimes, when it was my job to collect the mail, there would be a letter for Mum in distinctive handwriting. I quickly recognised that these letters were from Mum's friend Sister Ulrich, who lived in Queensland. Although, I didn't know much about Sister Ulrich, I looked forward to her mail, because sometimes there was something for me. The item I best remember is a 3D postcard, illustrated with koala bears. I thought it was absolutely fantastic.

Mum and Sister Ulrich wrote to each other fairly regularly and I formed the impression that Mum must have worked for her at some point. I also had the idea that Sister had looked out for Mum at some stage in her earlier life. Again, however, whenever I asked, there was never a satisfactory answer. When this happens often enough to a child, eventually, they just stop asking.

The daily newspaper *The West Australian* was also delivered. Mum was an avid reader, reading the newspaper from cover to cover. She even read the public notices.

At Caversham Primary School, most of the other pupils knew my Mum. She would turn up to school sports days and the annual Christmas concert .

After I moved on to Hampton Senior High School, Mum was not so obvious. The school was two bus rides from home and Mum still did not have a driver's licence. Back then, I was quite tiny, slim and thin-faced. With my dark hair and tan – we were always outside, even when we weren't at the beach – sometimes, I'd be asked whether I had any southern European heritage. Was I Italian? Or even Spanish? My stock answer was that I'd heard there was some Spanish blood way back in my Dad's line, but definitely no Italian. Around this time, my brother George had been given the nickname 'Mex'. Apparently, his features seemed Mexican to some of his schoolmates.

This must have affected me slightly, because even though it was popular back then for girls to have their ears pierced at around the age I was, I was determined never to have that done. Big hoop earrings were all the rage, but I didn't want to make myself look any more Italian than I already looked.

Also in high school, I was involved in an incident where a teacher was belittling a student. I defended the student, because I could not stand the way he had been singled out, for what I considered to be unfair treatment. Bullying and prejudice were issues that really riled me, though I was always careful to make a stand only when I felt that I was in a safe environment.

In this case, my outburst landed me in the office of the headmistress Miss Deidre Weston. She was quite an authoritarian figure and a lot of the girls found her intimidating. Miss Weston asked me to explain what had happened. I told her that the teacher had been making fun of my classmate and that I didn't think it was fair. To my huge surprise, Miss Weston agreed with me and I suffered no consequences.

By the time in 1977, when our family left our West Swan farm to move to a smaller block further south, I was the only York baby left at home. Dawn, Philip and George had already married by the time Mum, Dad and I made the move.

This all started when I made the choice to explore some of the questions that had remained unanswered. Questions that had been forming, since I was very young.

What was Sister Ulrich's connection to Mum?

Who was the mystery man in the wedding photograph, the man who gave my Mum's hand in marriage to Dad?

Who were the older ladies in the flash car, who used to visit Mum in the 1960s?

Who were my mother's family?

They were my family, too.

Who was she? Who am I?

2

'THE HAY STREET MALL INCIDENT'

– CR –

The event, that Jennifer and I now refer to as The Hay Street Mall Incident, happened in 1980. It was near the end of lunch, and I was heading back to work. For the past year or so, I'd been working as a journalist on *The Countryman*, a rural weekly magazine that was part of West Australian Newspapers Ltd (WAN). The band of lovable eccentrics that comprised *The Countryman* crew occupied the top floor of that grand old building, Newspaper House. The mall was heaving with shoppers and workers that day, jostling for space, rushing in all directions. As I quickened my pace, my gaze was drawn to one of the faces among the tidal wave of people that was thronging towards me. For the most fleeting of seconds, my mind formed the thought, 'That girl looks slightly Chinese'.

Moments later, I stood face to face with that girl Jennifer. She'd been heading back to the credit society, where she was starting a career in the banking industry. We only chatted briefly then as we were both in a tearing hurry, but we have since discussed that chance happening, way more deeply. Jennifer doesn't find it all that remarkable that I hadn't really thought much about how she looked, given her own earlier reactions to the portraits of her mother.

It may seem ludicrous that I had never really registered that my oldest friend had been blessed with a little exotic ethnicity. The fact is, we had known each other so long that I had never really seen what Jennifer looked like. I just saw Jennifer. Jennifer was three and I was four when we'd first encountered each other. I doubt that many kids of that age spend a lot of time intellectualising the ethnicity of a new friend. Our mothers and my grandmother had organised what these days would probably be called a play date. Back then, it was more a case of 'would you like to come down for a cup of tea?'

It was a fairly big day for me because it was the first time a girl had ever been to our place to play. And probably the last, come to think of it, until primary school when our worlds expanded considerably. Neither of our mothers drove a car at that stage. Like Marj, my Mum had also had several failed attempts to learn to drive on the old Caversham Airfield. For Jennifer and for me, home was the centre of our small universe.

To mark the occasion, the previous day, I'd persuaded Dad to help me build a seesaw. We rolled a big chock of wood away from the woodheap near the backyard dunny out onto the lawn under the clothesline. In those days, the clothesline was a length of wire between two bush poles, even the Hills Hoist was years off. Then Dad found a stout beam on one of the timber heaps and lay it across the chock. I thought it was wonderful and couldn't wait for this girl Jennifer to arrive and give it a go.

Mrs York and Jennifer arrived. They came down on the 9 o'clock bus that would have been taking the older members of the York brood down to Caversham Primary School. Back then, the old school was near the corner of Benara and West Swan Roads, about three miles towards Guildford.

Jennifer was something else. She had this massive grin and was as lively as a bag of crackers. Both physically and verbally. She didn't stop moving and nor did she stop talking.

Neither of us was the sort of little girl who was ever going to be content with sitting quietly on the floor, dressing dolls. So, while the women chatted and clinked china around the teapot, Jennifer and I buzzed around outside like two electrons.

Everyone seemed to be a Mrs or a Mr then out on the Swan. Even amongst themselves, first names were seldom used. Seniors were often granted the title Old Mr or Old Mrs and this was not a sign of disrespect, it was purely descriptive. Some may even have considered it flattery. Many of the senior Swan folk around then had survived at least one war, some two. They wore their age like a badge of honour.

I don't know that the seesaw was a great success, but Jennifer and I got on well enough. The meeting marked the start of our lifelong friendship. I felt disappointed when Grandad arrived back from Midland saleyards in his old red Chevy truck in time to give our visitors a lift home.

My grandparents lived north of where we did, about half way up the road to York's place. They had actually lived in the York house for a while in 1923, after they'd married, while they were waiting for their own house to be built. Our families were even distantly connected. Jennifer's aunt had married my grandmother's cousin.

Both had died even before our play date, but the connection would prove useful years later.

Occasionally, the York family would call into my grandparents' farm to buy fresh milk, though usually, this was fetched by the elder brother Philip on his bike with a billy can. It was after Jennifer started at Caversham Primary that we had the chance to get to know each other better.

It was 1964, when I was in Grade 3, in the middle room. Jennifer would have been in the junior room in Grade 2. We had a new headmaster that year, a tall, lean and fairly stern man. There were big windows down the west side of the middle room and I became aware of a bit of a ruckus happening outside. The headmaster, face like thunder, was marching from the junior room towards the big brick classroom, where the senior pupils toiled. Tucked under one arm was a writhing, squealing child. I recognised the child immediately. Jennifer was pummelling the headmaster with her fists, arms and legs flailing. He had her measure, but she wasn't going down without a fight.

She had every reason to put up some resistance. Waiting in the senior room were two of the older Yorks. Jennifer told me later that they couldn't run home fast enough after getting off the afternoon bus to report this fantastic news to their mother. Jennifer's crime? Talking, of course.

The Swan back then was a multicultural wonderland and nowhere was this more obvious than at that little primary school we attended. Just over 100 pupils, 114 in my final year and every family could tell a different story. Some of us were descended from soldiers who'd chosen to settle the fertile valley soils after World War I, others had fled war-ravaged Europe, in search of a better life. There were classmates who did not speak English at home. Some would start school with just a smattering of English at best. And yet, didn't they fly! Among the ranks of graduates, who may have stumbled through the unfamiliar territory that was Caversham back then, are fistfuls of degrees, doctorates and people who are articulate and engaging community and industry leaders in their chosen fields of endeavour. We may not have studied multiculturalism, but at Caversham we were living it.

Our neighbour made melt-in-the-mouth crostoli. One of the Caversham Mum's had once served me up baked cabbage rolls, filled with rice, mince and all sorts of herbs that set my taste buds on fire. Another family had sloshed red wine and water into my glass at the lunch table when I was about nine. This didn't happen at home. No-one was typical. Exceptions were the rule. Nowhere was this coming together of disparate parts more apparent than on the sports oval that extended to the bitumen playground, where we practised for weeks ahead of the annual athletics carnivals.

The headmaster loved athletics and fortunately, for Jennifer and me, it was a shared passion for us too. We were both sprinters. My idea of after-school entertainment was to see how fast I could fly along the cow tracks in the paddocks behind the house. Dad would get home from work some nights and find me at the front gate, ready to race the car down the track. We learned to never, ever look back. And never slow down when nearing the finishing tape, no matter how far ahead of the pack we might consider ourselves to be. Inattention like that could lose a race. Jennifer would get so excited before a race start that she would jump up and down very quickly on the spot, sometimes vocalising as well, releasing some of her abundant nervous energy. It wasn't intended to spook the opposition, but some may have found it unsettling. She was incredibly fast, her long plaits flying. Our middle primary teacher nicknamed her The Flying Pigtails.

Parents would often turn up to support us and it was after one of the athletics carnivals that she experienced her first and last racist taunt at Caversham. She didn't see it as prejudice back then just a couple of silly boys being really annoying. These particular boys must have noticed that her Mum looked Chinese and said so, adding a few jibes. Jennifer was the youngest of four and no shrinking violet. I remember my grandfather telling me when she would have been around this age that he liked her 'because she calls a spade a spade'. 'What did you do?' I asked when she recounted the taunts.

'I beat them up,' she said. 'They never worried me again.'

Another time, Jennifer stood up for a boy from one of the vineyard families when another boy was grandstanding, trying to convince everyone that his family was a cut above the other boy's. Jennifer stepped in and stopped it. She was always a champion of the underdog, and never had any patience for prejudice in any form.

When Jennifer and I moved on to high school, our conversation time lengthened, mainly because it meant catching two buses, with a twenty-minute wait, outside our old primary school, for the connecting bus down West Swan Road each afternoon.

One of those rides home provided a memorable test of the friendship. Jennifer was glowing, when I slipped into the seat beside her. She'd obviously had a good day from the look on her face, almost incandescent. As the bus droned along Beechboro Road and into Benara, she told me that at lunch time she and her good mate Gail had escaped the school grounds and headed for the corner telephone box. This worried me a bit. What if they'd been seen?

They'd broken a school rule and the reigning head mistress was a strict disciplinarian.

Jennifer wasn't at all bothered. She just stared out of the window, as if in some sort of victory trance, relating how they'd dialled some poor hapless individual, pretended to be from a Perth radio station and posed the question, 'How many holes in a crumpet?' Their victim had made a wild stab at the answer, they'd announced that the guess was spot on and had promised there'd soon be a prize in the post. A pair of pantyhose. I loftily thought it all sounded a bit juvenile, until Jennifer dropped the name of the person they'd called. My mother!

The cold stone in the pit of my stomach had grown to a rock as I dragged myself up the track towards the house that night. And chewed on a dry vegemite sandwich, feeling as sick as I'd ever felt before any sports carnival. Mum, however, was unusually buoyant. She told me she'd successfully answered a question on a radio quiz and was expecting a new pair of pantyhose to arrive. Any day. She repeated the story of her success that night, after Dad came home. We were at dinner and I can't recall exactly what we were eating, but it sat as dry and unappetising as the Tuesday night rissoles we'd have, during the time we killed our own sheep. Sunday's huge roast lamb would become Monday night's cold meat and boiled vegetables, with the leftovers pummelled through the mincer and mixed with egg to form the sort of rissoles that stuck hard in the gut on Tuesdays.

I didn't dare look at Dad, especially when Mum got to the 'how many holes in a crumpet?' bit. Dad was the youngest of three brothers. He was perhaps a little more street savvy than Mum. Out of the corner of one eye, I felt his lips may have twitched just a little. The incident remained our little secret and I never did spill the beans. Mum's pantyhose never did arrive either and she lost a bit of puff, as the week wore on. But I don't think she ever suspected she'd been duped. Not by Jennifer at least. It was only a tiny secret. And every family had them.The Swan was no different. Privacy was respected. We all had stories. If someone was reluctant to discuss an event in their lives, no-one was ever going to shine a bright light in their face and demand answers. Besides, no-one was drifting around thinking too much. There was always so much to do.

After school, when Jennifer and I were younger, we spent a lot of time fishing and gilgying (gilgies are a freshwater crayfish) in Wandoo Creek at my grandparents' place. Back then, the water teemed with river fish, tadpoles as big as gum nuts, leeches that stuck to our calves and nipping river shrimps.

Later, the Yorks included me on some of their fishing trips further afield. Early morning excursions, south to Boggy Bay near Pinjarra, wading the water for crabs. Then that memorable fishing trip to Burns Beach in January 1980. Everyone had packed up ready to leave, all except Marj, who was still in the water with a sizeable wobbegong that had just snapped the line.

Marj seemed so at home in the water, she didn't appear fazed. It's the set look on Henry's face that I most clearly remember. Arms pumping, eyes focused ahead, he raced down the sand and into the churning foam like a man possessed.

Mr and Mrs York were Marj and Henry to me by this stage. Often, Marj and I would head off to the football together in my little orange Honda. We were both Swan Districts tragics. Jennifer didn't join us. Her Mum had dragged her along one too many times, when she was younger. On one memorable occasion, Jennifer had been so put off by her mother's enthusiastic barracking that she'd finished up, right at the top of the McDonald Stand, quietly reading *Wuthering Heights*.

Marj's enthusiasm didn't worry me. Though the quietly spoken homemaker I thought I knew certainly transformed, once the siren sounded to start play. Someone once accused Marj of being a one-eyed Swans supporter. But my Dad defended her,'Marj isn't one-eyed, she has two eyes,' he'd said. 'One white and one black.'

In May 1975, Jennifer's sister Dawn married Jim, and a few weeks before the event, Jennifer told me they were expecting an interstate guest. Sister Ulrich (now Mrs Ulrich, as she had long retired from nursing) was making the trip from Nambour in Queensland, by coach, to be at the wedding. Mrs Ulrich was in her mid-seventies and stayed in the York home for a couple of weeks, sharing Jennifer's room. Jennifer recalls she was fairly frail, with poor eyesight and hearing, and had a passion for Cool Mints.

It must have been quite an effort for that frail, elderly woman to undertake such a long and gruelling road trip, to catch up with the family of an old friend. Perhaps it was an indication of her regard for Marj? If so, where did that regard stem from? How were the two women connected? The visit did apparently provide an opportunity for Mrs Ulrich and Henry York to make peace after Philip's difficult delivery in 1949.

Mrs Ulrich, a midwife, was in Perth, at the time of the birth. Henry had become increasingly concerned for Marj's welfare after a three-day labour, which appeared to not be progressing. He'd pleaded with the medical team, 'Take the baby, and save my wife.' Mrs Ulrich apparently strongly disagreed with this and in due course, Philip was born safely. The disagreement, which had apparently hung between

Mrs Ulrich and Henry since 1949, was publicly put right at Dawn and Jim's wedding reception twenty-six years later.

Her parting gift to Jennifer was a copy of the Bible. Inside the front cover, in her distinctive handwriting, she'd written a note of thanks. She expressed her gratitude at having been able to share Jennifer's room and added a reference from the Bible. Religious Education had been one of the subjects back at Caversham, but I don't remember Jennifer being there. She was in the group that skipped Scripture for supervised private study, as her Dad reckoned his kids could make their own choices about religion, when they were older.

Jennifer said, 'I took the Bible down to your place, and we tried to work out the significance of the quote, but neither of us really had a clue. We just decided it must have meant something about sharing'.

Recently, when we were discussing The Hay Street Mall Incident, she reminded me of a similar incident that had happened during her time working at the Shire of Swan offices. She'd been assigned switchboard duty, taking calls and putting callers through to the appropriate departments, when a caller rang in who claimed to know her. Jennifer said she didn't recognise the voice at all, nor the accent, both of which were distinctive. The caller was adamant that they knew her. Jennifer was just as adamant that she hadn't a clue who was on the other end of the line.

'Just tell me, who is this!' she finally demanded.

'Jennifer, it's your mother,' Marj calmly replied.

Marj did have an almost musical lilt, a singsong melody to her manner of speech. Even her way of pronouncing Jen-nif-er, broke the name into three syllables. One of the most distinctive features of Marj's accent was her inability to pronounce the *v* sound, which was substituted with a *b*. Hence, vegetables became begetables and she could never properly say the name of one of our Swan neighbours, the Viskovich family.

By now, Jennifer was about to start asking a lot more questions. One of the responses she would get from Marj was that she had spoken Chinese exclusively until she was about six years old. That made sense. So that would explain Marj's accent. Wouldn't it?

3

THE COACH BACK FROM CALAIS

– JD –

It was up the back of the coach, returning to London from Calais, that I made two of the most important decisions of my life. Three, if you also count the decision to go back to Australia, rather than stay longer overseas, try to find work and travel more, as the others now planned to do. This was 31 July 1981. I was coming to the end of two months in England, Scotland and Europe. My first really big trip overseas and the longest time I'd ever been away from home.

My travelling companions were my old friend Cheryl and two girls from her year at the high school that we'd all attended. I didn't know Lindy and Leanne all that well before we'd left home in early June. But in the past weeks, we'd shared a lot of cheap hotel rooms, hostel dormitories and adventures.

In Hong Kong, Lindy, Cheryl and I had caught public buses out to the border with China. We caught up with Leanne in London and spent a couple of weeks driving around England and Scotland in a hire car. Other drivers would toot at us. It probably had something to do with the clothesline we'd strung up across inside the back, to dry our undies.

We took a homemade Aussie flag to the First Ashes Test, at Trent Bridge in Nottingham, and screamed for Lillee, Marsh, Alderman and the rest of the Australians until bad light stopped play. On our 19-day tour of Europe, I'd danced on a table at a fondue night in Lucerne. The table had collapsed, but luckily, a quick-thinking man broke my fall. At the Sistine Chapel, we'd all hired sound recordings and lay on our backs on the floor, looking up at Michelangelo's frescoes on the ceiling. In Florence, the sun had come out just as we got to the statue of David and it lit up the marble. The tour was coming to an end and we'd all been talking about our plans for the future. Lindy and I were up the back of the coach, everyone else was asleep. The topic of Mum came up and by this time, I felt I knew Lindy a lot better.

I told her I needed to do two things. The first was to find out Mum's history, as we really knew nothing about her until she'd met Dad. They'd become engaged in September 1947 and married the following April, when she was 23, the age I was then.

I could not believe that someone could be on this earth for that length of time without any trace. By this stage, I had already asked Mum about her family and where she came from. Whenever I asked, she would give me a little bit of information and then she would cry. I hated upsetting her, so I would stop asking until the next time.

The second major decision I'd made was to make contact with a young man I'd met, a few weeks before we'd left for England. Geoffrey Durrant was friends with a group of girls I'd been at high school with. They'd all left at the end of Third Year, whereas I'd stayed on. He was the guy they asked, whenever they needed a no-strings partner to go to a wedding. Geoff was a very good dancer, his parents had insisted all their kids take lessons. I was useless. One of the girls Liz was having a party. They'd asked Geoffrey and they asked me. I think they were trying to set us up together. They thought we had the same sense of humour. I'm not sure if we talked at that party, but when I was heading for my car, in the early hours of the next morning, I heard someone call out 'Oi!' Geoff was trying to sleep, in the back seat of his station wagon. He'd probably had a drink or two, and did not want to drive. He was a good boy. I walked over to his window and we chatted for a while, but it was getting cold outside. Really cold!

'Move over. I'm coming in,' I told him and climbed through the open back window.

We started chatting and talked for ages, until I said it was time I went home. Geoff and I went out for a few weeks after that, but I had this overseas trip planned. I was feeling really excited about something, but I really didn't know whether I was feeling excited about getting to know Geoff or whether it was just because I was about to head overseas. Also, although I'd booked leave from work, I wasn't really sure at that stage whether I'd just travel for a few weeks and come home. Or would I want to stay longer? The other girls were talking about it. In the end, I took Geoff on a picnic and I let him go.

But up the back of the coach that day, I decided to get back in touch with Geoff once I was home. He did have a great sense of humour. And he had great legs! Maybe it was the dancing. He also played and coached cricket out in the Swan Valley, on the other side of the river to where I'd grown up. I didn't want to die wondering what might have been.

It was the same with trying to find out more about Mum.

I only had a few more days with the girls before it was time to fly home. Despite the cold, I was determined to fit in a swim, off a crunchy beach at Weymouth. The others were not so keen. We talked until midnight on my last night, then the girls dropped me off at Gatwick, to catch the flight home. That was on Friday, 7 August 1981.

Not long after I got back, Mum and Dad headed up north. Nearly every winter after Dad retired until he died in 1988, they would take off in their little yellow and white caravan to go fishing. They usually camped somewhere in the area around Exmouth, so they would have travelled through Carnarvon on the way there. They'd be away for a couple of months. Dad was meticulous about packing. He'd even made a frame for the boat to sit in the back of his ute. They'd take a deep freeze and generator, they liked to be as self-sufficient as possible, living mainly off the fish they caught. That left me home alone. So, while they were away that year, 1981, I called Geoff and invited him to dinner. The rest, as they say, is history. Mum told me later that she'd had a dream, a premonition, while they were up north. It was that Geoff and I had got back together. She'd dreamed it the same night that Geoff had come over. Mum was quite a spiritual person. She once had a premonition that one of my brothers had been involved in a car accident. And he had. Fortunately, he was not seriously hurt. She was also very religious. At some stage in her life, she had done bible studies, I knew that. It must have been just after this time that I also asked Mum more questions about what she knew about her own past.

I'd invested in a new 200-page Bowater Reporter notebook to keep a record of any findings. The more common style of this sort of notebook had a yellow cover, a style I associated with work, so I went for one with a cover in two tones of blue instead. I was pretty confident that I'd have all the answers I needed, fairly soon.

I still have the blue notebook and it's dated 1981. It must have been between August and December that year, because I didn't get back to Australia until early August. Those early entries were written with a fountain pen, a sign of the importance I placed on the information. Some of the entries I made then would make little sense to me. Not for a long, long time.

I have corrected some of the misspellings and added more information, based on what I would later learn:

- 25 November 1924 (not confirmed) (This was the date we'd always assumed was Mum's birth date, although she did not have a birth certificate to prove it was correct);
- Born in Derby;
- Attended Lawley Ladies' College in Mt Lawley. There had been a bank book, in the name of Marjorie King, Mum's name before she'd married. It was for a Commonwealth Bank branch in Mt Lawley. We'd gone down together to the bank to close the account, which I gathered dated from her days as a student at the College;
- Used to fly between Carnarvon and Perth in flying boats, during World War II. I assumed this was to travel to and from school in Perth;
- Josephine (dead);
- Auntie Una (just called Auntie – dead);
- King Wee Quan Sing (I would later learn the correct alternative spellings were 'Kingwell/Kinwell/Kinevell', and he was known as Nugget);
- Ken Quan Sing (Kenton or Kinton);
- Winston Quan Sing (Winson);
- Gary Quan Sing;

- A small boy named Gary, hurt in an explosion, possibly the same Gary as above;
- Fishing off the jetty in Carnarvon;
- Eating oysters off the reef in Carnarvon;
- Waterfront shops;
- Plantation;
- Shark bite on the knee when aged about 15;
- A piece of tin thrown into left eye;
- Showed me a photograph of Carnarvon in the floods;
- Knew her father was called Lanky (a nickname, real name Kinverns), and he was a Quan Sing;
- Remembered sitting on the back step, listening to the men whispering, speaking Chinese.

It wasn't much to go on, but I had to start somewhere.

I found the name Quan Sing in the telephone book, and decided to try my luck, first with an unannounced visit to a couple who lived about 20 minutes away. Mum knew nothing of this. I was unbelievably nervous that day, setting out with my blue notebook. How would these people react when I told them my mother believed her father was possibly a close relative of theirs? As I walked towards the door, I noticed a little car parked out the front. It had Carnarvon number plates. It seemed a good sign. At least, I probably had the right family. A dark-haired woman, in her sixties, answered the door. Somehow, I blurted out the introduction I'd rehearsed.

'Hi, my name is Jennifer. I believe that my mother may be related to the Quan Sings. She believes that her father had the nickname Lanky.'

The woman was Lily Quan Sing, wife of one of Lanky's younger brothers, Kingwell, whose nickname was Nugget. She didn't seem to register any surprise at what I'd said. Her husband's late brother Kinverns had been called Lanky she told me. But she didn't know whether or not he'd had any children out of wedlock. She had not heard any rumours to that effect. Lily also told me that her husband couldn't help me either, as he'd suffered a stroke which had left him unable to speak, but she invited me in.

When I walked in and saw Kingwell, it was obvious to me why he'd been given the nickname Nugget. He would have been in his late seventies by this stage, and was confined to a wheelchair, but I could see he was a big man, who must have had a powerful build when he was younger.

Lily listened, as I read out the list of information I'd noted down from my few talks with Mum about her past. She was able to confirm that Gary was their son. They also had another son Colin who has since passed away and a daughter Julie, who is close to my age.

The Quan Sings had been storekeepers in Derby, before moving to Carnarvon, where Kingwell had a banana plantation. Lily was also able to tell me that Lanky had run the family store in Carnarvon with help from his brothers Ken and Winson. He had married late in life to a nurse called Pauline, who was a sister at the Carnarvon Hospital. But Lanky had died, many years ago, and she didn't know what had happened to Pauline.

Lily said that the information Mum had given me all made sense to her, but she could not remember Mum. Not at all. I found this almost unbelievable. Mum had provided such specific details – names, events, places – she must have been there. Why had they not noticed her? But I had the same response when I phoned Ken, who lived in Karrinyup. He was a quietly spoken, serious man. He told me he wouldn't be surprised to know that Lanky had fathered a child, but he had not heard of it. He could shed no light on it at all and he didn't remember a small girl called Marjorie King either.

Winson was still living in Carnarvon, running the family store. He was the youngest of that big Quan Sing family and seemed quite cheery and open when I called him out of the blue. He struck me as being quite a whimsical character. 'I wouldn't be surprised,' was his reaction, when I said it was possible Lanky was my mother's father. He had a slight accent, but not like Mum's, he sounded pretty Aussie. He too listened, as I read out the list of Mum's recollections. 'If your mother knew all these people, then she must be related. But I don't remember her at all.'

Winson was born in 1920, just four years before Mum. Surely, being so close in age, they'd have known each other, played together? But like everyone else I'd asked, he seemed genuinely puzzled by what I'd told him.

I was devastated. I'd stuck my neck out and got nowhere. There seemed no point in contacting any of the younger generation of Quan Sings. If Lanky's brothers didn't remember Mum, they would be even less likely to have any information that might help. I tossed the notebook in the bottom of my undies drawer and forgot about it. For a while.

Besides, I had enough to do. Work was keeping me very busy. So was Geoff and things were getting serious. One Friday night, he came in to pick me up. He hadn't been to my work before, and at that stage, he'd not met anyone from there. He'd only heard about them, from me.

My workmates were very protective of me, being one of the younger members of staff, and they were curious about this young man I was seeing. They almost ate Geoff alive. They gave him the third degree, even asking what his intentions were. He was really traumatised by the experience, but at least it didn't put him off completely.

We were married on 8 January 1983. Cheryl had come home from England, a few weeks before and she and Gail from high school were my best women. I can't stand the term bridesmaid. Geoff was also pretty busy at work. He's a cabinet-maker and later would have his own business.

When we were newly married, Mum made Geoff and me four top sheets for our bed. She used calico and at first, they felt really scratchy, it was like sleeping under stiff sandpaper. But once the calico softened, they were soft as, and not too hot, not too cold. We still have two of the four left, 38 years later.

Building our first house took up more time and it was 20 August 1985 before I looked at the blue notebook again. This time, I made a note of the date on one of the pages. Cheryl had returned to England early in 1984 and was still there when I had this second burst of activity.

Meanwhile, in November 1984, Mum turned 60 and we surprised her with a party at Dawn and Jim's. Her old friends from out on the Swan were there, as well as our family. We gave her a string of pearls. My sister Dawn is now the 'keeper of Mum's pearls' and wears them whenever we have a York family gathering.

At this point, I still had no real clues about what Mum's life had been like before her marriage. The York house had quite a few photographs of us kids together, family portraits, posing with our new station wagon, loaded up with show bags at the Perth Royal Show. Where were the photographs of Mum as a girl?

In August 1985, I contacted the Registry of Births, Deaths and Marriages, to request a copy of Mum's birth certificate. I provided her date of birth, 25 November 1924, her name Marjorie King and her place of birth Derby. The staff there were really helpful when nothing showed up after the first search, they searched all the records for the Derby area around that time. And they found nothing, I had a letter back to say that there was no official record of Mum's birth.

Then I contacted the Shire of Carnarvon. And drew another blank. The official word there was that all records had been destroyed in the 1965 floods. Finding any record of pupils who'd attended Carnarvon Primary School, around the time Mum should have been there, was just as hard. The original school had been knocked down 10 years before my inquiry and the records were destroyed with it.

Then I tried to chase up some information about Lawley Ladies' College. But all I came up with was Lady Lawley Cottage in Cottesloe. It didn't seem like the right place and Cottesloe was a long way from Mt Lawley where Mum had an account with the local branch of the Commonwealth Bank. Next I contacted Carnarvon Hospital's administration. Maybe they'd have a record of Pauline Quan Sing, or even Sister Ulrich, if she'd worked there. But this was all hopeless, I was told no records had been kept.

After this, I called Lily Quan Sing again to see if she or any other members of the family had remembered anything else after my visit. But she had nothing new to report to me. 'Nugget' Quan Sing passed away in December 1985.

Beneath the note about having made contact with Lily, I'd written the name L.T. Chiew and a telephone number. Or perhaps, that was why I'd written the name Burrows, a few lines further down. Was this a line of inquiry opened up by the mysterious L.T. Chiew?

I had made a note of the date later when again I called Winson Quan Sing on 2 May 1986. I mentioned the name Burrows and

Winson told me he believed Lanky and a Mrs Burrows had had an affair. Her husband had found out and he hadn't been very happy. He mentioned the name Burrows but was not certain about Mrs Burrows' first name. He thought maybe it could have been Florence. He did seem pretty certain that Mrs Burrows had become pregnant at around the time she'd had the alleged relationship with Lanky.

The next entry in my blue notebook records a telephone call I'd received from a woman called Pat Bird. It was the second time I'd spoken to Mrs Bird, who knew a lot about Carnarvon history. This time, she told me more about what she knew of the relationship between Lanky and Mrs Burrows.

Pat Bird phoned today to say Lanky used to sometimes deliver vegetables to Mrs Burrows. Usually, his offsider did the deliveries, when Lanky would deliver to them, Mr Burrows went off his head.

She too was not absolutely certain about names. It was all such a long time ago. Her recollection was that Mr and Mrs Burrows had left town, around 1923, the year before Mum was born. That's if the information Mum had about her date of birth was correct.

This was all turning out to be a lot harder than I'd thought. There were so many dead ends. Every question I asked seemed only to throw up more questions. Nothing was adding up. I stuffed the blue notebook back in the bottom of the drawer.

Meanwhile, Geoff and I were facing other challenges. Just after I'd turned 30, we went through a couple of IVF procedures. I'd had a few health issues for years and the process ended up consuming an awful lot of our lives. Unfortunately, the procedures were not successful.

My Dad died in December 1988 after a short illness which left Mum alone, needing a little more family support. She did go on to pass that driving test though, eventually. By this time, she was in her mid-sixties. It took 28 lessons, several attempts and a lot of deep breathing for me! Mum enjoyed more independence in her later life, partly because of her driver's licence and also her love of travel. She went on numerous escorted tours, seeing places all around Australia. By 1999, when Mum was nearing her mid-seventies, we decided it might be better if she moved a little closer to the family, so we could help provide her with more support. She sold the house in Tomlin Street, West Swan, and moved into a half-duplex, which happened to come onto the market at the time we were looking. It was conveniently located, right around the corner from where Geoff and I were living in Eden Hill. We had to drive past it whenever we went out and came home.

Mum was still driving her little white hatchback at this stage but missed out on her licence when she took her practical test late 2000 and on her birthday that year, she had to hang up her keys. It didn't stop her travelling though. That same November, she flew to Sydney and saw the sights of Canberra and Melbourne, before heading for Kangaroo Island, on another escorted tour. Mum remained living independently until late 2004. Her left eye gave her trouble. It used to weep quite a bit and Mum blamed this on the damage caused, when she was young, when some older children had teased her and one had thrown a jagged piece of tin at her eye. She was always dabbing at it with a tissue, or a hanky. Eventually, a cataract developed and had to be removed.

She had started having a few falls, had osteoarthritis and in December that year, was admitted to Hollywood Hospital, suffering from pain in her back. She was still in hospital, the following January 2005, when scans revealed she had a small fracture in her spine. It was obvious by this stage that Mum could not go back to her duplex. We settled on a care facility in Yokine, not far from Dawn and Jim and Mum moved from Hollywood into aged care on January 31. Although Mum was to live another two and a half years and remained at the centre of family events, the odds were stacking against her. In late June, 2007, she had major surgery from which she never recovered. In early July, she entered palliative care and Dawn and Jim made a mercy dash home from a holiday in Queensland, arriving just in time to say their goodbyes before Mum passed away in the early hours of Monday, 9 July.

Around the time of her passing, in the early hours of the morning, I had dreamt that Dad had come to get her. I was at the hospital by 5.30am, but she had already gone. She loved nothing more than her children, grandchildren and great-grandchildren. Towards the end of her life, she had been in a lot of pain and was not able to get around as much, but her face would always beam when she saw the little ones.

The week after Mum's death was the longest seven days of my life. We had to wait, for all the grandkids to be in Perth. Dawn and Jim's daughter was in the eastern states with soccer and school commitments and Philip's daughter was FIFO.

Mum's funeral service, the Monday after her passing, was well attended with her children, grandchildren and great-grandchildren paying tribute, along with her many friends from her days out on the Swan.

Things didn't go quite so smoothly when we had to make a decision about Mum's final resting place. Dawn and I, as executors, discussed a number of options, but neither of us felt comfortable with many on the list. The little church, up the road from our old West Swan farm, seemed right, but we were unable to place Mum's ashes there because the regulations at the time would not allow it. I was a bit upset about this, we were getting nowhere.

In the end, Mum's ashes, in their beautiful jarrah box, went on to the bookshelves Geoff had made that lined one wall of our front room. There they would remain, for 11 years. When our beloved Jack Russell Riley died, his ashes went up on the shelf next to Mum's. They'd been great mates, so it seemed right. Whenever I dusted in that room, I'd touch the boxes and say a few words to them both.

With such a lot happening on so many different levels of my life throughout this time, the blue notebook stayed safe in the bottom of that undies drawer for pretty much 27 years. Until 2013, when everything began to change. The gods had been sleeping. Now they were starting to wake up.

4

FAMILY SECRETS, TRUTHS AND LIES

– CR –

For all the years that Jennifer's blue notebook was tucked away in its drawer, I'd been unearthing our own family's secrets. Gaining the sort of knowledge that you'd think might be useful to help in her quest, eventually.

Less than three weeks before Lindy, Jennifer and I flew out for London, my maternal grandmother Vera Day, had died. As a young bride, she had lived in the house where Jennifer's family had lived, when we were children. My grandmother had been a huge part of my life, growing up. She and her two surviving sisters, Ida and Lila, would get together often, to exchange armloads of their homegrown silverbeet, shallots, jams, milk, cream, plant cuttings or whatever else happened to be in abundant supply. Inevitably, they'd gather around the table and talk would turn to family stories. They were skilled archivists and keepers of history.

They'd squawk with laughter, recounting stories, like the comedy of their brother and cousin looking after the minister's horse at a Middle Swan Church. The congregation had spilled out and observed the horse still hitched in the shafts in front of the sulky, but it was facing the wrong way.

In World War I, they'd lost a much-loved older brother, Harold. He was the 1915 Rhodes scholar for Western Australia, killed in a flying accident in 1916, while training with the Royal Flying Corps. They kept his light burning, recalling how he'd taught them the steps to dances, finishing under the kitchen table because the house was so small.

Their stories embraced names and details, beyond our immediate families of Haddrills and Whitemans. This would have been where I'd learned about the connection between our Haddrills and Jennifer's York line. Grandma had looked after two of the Haddrill boys, after their mother Etta (nee York) died unexpectedly and prematurely. Etta was Henry York's sister, Jennifer's aunt.

There were stories, ones that had never been written down, but passed down through word of mouth from mother to daughter. I'd always been around the edge of the table, as they talked, soaking it in. Their stories were as rich and colourful as the embroidery stitched into the starched tablecloths that they insisted upon using.

Later, I would appreciate how this experience had informed me about the people who had shaped my place in the world. Jennifer had none of this on her maternal side. Whereas, I'd been endlessly drip-fed names, dates and anecdotes, she'd heard only silence. Little wonder, her curiosity would build up over the years. When Marj and I went to the football, to cheer on the Swans, often, Aunt Lila's husband Uncle Harry would go too, even driving us to matches in his Kombi. Aunt Lila was the youngest and the chief record-keeper. She catalogued old photographs, kept newspaper clippings and wrote articles about the Swan she'd once known, which even then was fast disappearing.

She also corresponded regularly with her cousin in England, Una Whiteman. Lila once told me that her father had strongly encouraged her, even insisted, that she maintain contact with her English cousins. Otherwise, there was the risk that the family connection would be lost. Una was the go-to person in that particular line. She knew more about our connections than most of us knew ourselves. I was looking forward to meeting her when I could get down to her home in Bexhill on Sea, in East Sussex.

First, I had to earn a living in London. I found a few week's work as a temporary secretary. So, began my life as a temp, filling in, whenever someone's annual leave, work overload or grumbling appendix might call.

Down the Portobello Road markets, I bought an old blue bike and would ride it to work in Victoria, where a firm of engineers had one floor of a building, opposite Buckingham Palace Mews. The more I ventured, the further I yearned to explore London's tiny alleyways and back streets, parks that changed with each season, and its people. I sought out characters, like London cabbies, for stories to send off to travel magazines.

I was starting to dip my toes in the waters of a city that had at first seemed overwhelming, almost threatening, with its surging crowds, its noise, the sheer rush of it all. Civil unrest was also rife and unfamiliar, the only city I'd worked in until then was Perth. Yet here I was, amidst transport strikes, riots in Brixton and beyond, and it was a particularly active time for the Irish Republican Army (IRA).

None of this was written about in letters home. There is no mention of strife, of protest marches, nor is there any hint of nail bombs or the explosives officer who lost his life, trying to defuse a bomb in a hamburger outlet on Oxford Street. Nowhere do I mention the Troubles.

I'd been trained in the era of old school journalism. Present the facts and let the readers decide. Don't editorialise. Yet, I was just as capable of censoring the truth and of creating an elegant spin as the slickest PR campaigner. The things we do for love.

One weekend, I got away to East Sussex and met up with Una Whiteman. She didn't disappoint. I still think of her as our very own Miss Marple and how lucky we were to have had such an enthusiastic and generous sleuth. She brought out vast charts where she'd plotted family lines and connections in her neat, schoolteacher's hand. We pored over black and white photographs and old letters. She'd even found one, written by my great-uncle Harold to one of his aunts.

There were numerous surprising moments that weekend. One of our shared ancestors had apparently not been the person she had seemed to be. Una's methodical research had uncovered that my great great-grandmother was the result of an affair between her mother and a publican, but this information had not been presented when she married. A different history had been created instead.

Did she do this because she felt a sense of shame, we wondered? Did she even know her father's identity? Perhaps she only knew what she had been told. Her secret would have remained our assumption of truth but for Una's diligence. I left with copious notes, more information about some of the souls who had helped shape me. Una had also taught me some valuable lessons about never simply assuming that the obvious was necessarily correct.

That spring, I took a few days off work to collect my grandfather Walter Day from Heathrow. He'd flown in with friends to spend time with his sister's family in East Anglia. One day, in London, we took a river boat down the Thames to the pub where Grandad had drunk a beer before sailing for Australia 70 years before, in 1912, when he was 21. We had lunch and bus-hopped back to Kensington before heading to Victoria Coach Station, where he boarded a coach back to East Anglia.

As a child, I had been his shadow, walking the high rail at Midland saleyards, yarding cattle, building a timber gate together, priming windmills, watching cricket. My first driving lessons were on his old grey Fergie.

The contrast between what I knew of my maternal line because communication was key and I had access to the people or at least people who remembered those who'd come before, would help me better understand when Jennifer's quest for information grew from a niggling interest into near obsession.

My parents had caught up with Jennifer and Geoff who were also getting pretty serious. My mother was so excited that she took the plastic covers off the not-so-new-now lounge suite for the event. Dad reported that Geoff was a Swan Districts Football Club supporter, adding the comment, 'That will please Marj.' Marj was certainly a great fan of the Fighting Swans, as they were called back then. When the club won back-to-back premierships in 1961, 1962 and 1963, she was ecstatic. When the Club went through a long losing streak, Marj had telephoned and offered advice to a trainer, 'You need to give the boys more beach training. It will build up their leg muscles. They play like they're tired.'

I returned home, at the end of 1982 and went back to rural journalism, hoping one day to return and work on a paper, somewhere like Salisbury or Cambridge. That was the dream. The timing worked out well because Jennifer and Geoff's wedding was early in 1983. They hadn't wasted much time. She always was quick out of the blocks.

We all got together again, early 1984, about one month before I returned overseas. Jennifer had done her first round of Quan Sing interviews by this stage, but her second stage of inquiry would happen after I'd gone.

I'd always done a bit of freelancing and kept this up in London, writing travel stories and legging it off to medical conferences, seminars about agriculture, keeping the wolf from the door. Then, a job came up for a press officer in North Wales. Working the season at a Butlin's Holiday Centre from April to September. Time passed quickly in a haze of glamorous grandmothers, beautiful babies, fancy-dress competition winners, visits by the Welsh lifeguards, ballroom dancing championships, trips down slate mines and guest appearances by past Olympians and soccer stars.

Staff had one day off each week on a Saturday. I used that time to see as much of North Wales as could be had, on a daily bus pass. One trip was to Portmeirion, an Italianate tourist village that had inspired filmmakers and writers, including Noel Coward. It had also been used as the village setting for the television series *The Prisoner*, starring Patrick McGoohan.

On the day of my visit, the others roaming the grounds and wild gardens that included colourful banks of rhododendrons and azaleas were all speaking a guttural, Germanic-sounding language. I assumed they were German tourists and felt a little bit more local with one line of my ancestors having lived in South Wales.

But when I got back to the office, our passionate Welsh national photographer Trefor Davies had set me straight. 'They were speaking

Welsh!' he told me, laughing and shaking his head. He added that there were still some people in the more remote villages of that rugged mountain landscape who were exclusive Welsh speakers, known as monoglot Welsh. And there was a growing push by many to preserve the language, before it disappeared.

When the season finished, I found a basement bedsit in Cambridge, retrieved the old blue bike that my East Anglian kin had kept safe and took a job as a secretary at Addenbrooke's Hospital.

Shared morning and afternoon tea breaks were mandatory. The powers that be recognised that effective communication was key. Scientists were strongly encouraged to get out of their laboratories where many worked in comparative isolation and talk to one another.

The same attitude had prevailed at the old Newspaper House in Perth, where I'd started out as a cadet journalist, on *The Countryman*. So much of my education in journalism came from shared conversations around the tea table in the vast, staff canteen.

Later, we'd moved to a flash new building, with a scaled-down canteen, and tea and coffee-making facilities, provided in a small space, on every floor. The thinking was that this was more efficient. Staff would take their tea or coffee back to their desks and keep working. I still feel that journalism lost something in that era. The sense of connection, chance to reboot and a forum for sharing story ideas had been diminished.

While I was working in Cambridge, researcher and immunologist César Milstein was named joint winner of the 1984 Nobel Prize for Medicine. I took an hour off work to attend the press conference, phoned the story through to *New Scientist* from a public phone box, and went back to work. New Scientist paid £25, one week's rent was £23.50.

A job as a journalist on the *Cambridge Weekly News* series of newspapers came up and provided the perfect keyhole into the world of town and gown, and beyond. The upstairs floor of the Newmarket Road headquarters was a cosy place of warm and friendly people, enthusiastic, knowledgeable and nurturing.

My grandfather Walter Day who I'd grown up with, had lived on a farm in the Cambridgeshire Fens until he was 21. Two lines of my father's family also hailed from the county. Dad's maternal grandmother had set out from Haddenham to find work as a housemaid in neighbouring Cottenham, 12 kilometres away. This was in 1874, Mothering Sunday and she was twelve. Today, this walk would take two hours and 23 minutes.

Sarah Matilda 'Tilly' Porter had found work that day and it led to her also finding a husband. Six years later, aged 18, and eight months pregnant, she'd married her employer's farmer son. He was 31. They would go on to have five more children, in a love match that endured, until her husband's death. I'd heard this story many times before coming to Cambridge. Little wonder, I felt so at home there.

Curiosity would inevitably lead me to seek out the Cambridgeshire Collection at the county library. The Local Studies Librarian, Chris Jakes, had been working in the collection since 1976. He was from the same Fenland village as my grandfather and had a special interest in Cambridgeshire men who had emigrated and fought for Commonwealth countries in World War I. I was happy to share the facts and photographs about my grandfather, knowing it would be stored for future generations to access. In return, Chris introduced me to a wealth of records, trade directories and old newspapers, available on microfiche to the public. In one old newspaper, there was a report of my grandfather being awarded a Military Medal. It told me the award was for conspicuous bravery on the Western Front, by bringing in the wounded.

We had always known about the award as he had the medal, but he would never speak about the circumstances. 'It was a terrible time, love. You don't want to know about it,' had been his gentle but firm rebuke, the only time I'd asked. This from a person, to whom I had always felt so close. Even Grandad had his secrets. I'd felt just a little bit hurt, but I'd never asked him again. Like Jennifer with Marj, I knew not to push too far.

Chris Jakes gave the following good-natured but telling advice. 'If you study local or national history, always check your references. Never believe anything in print and if you publish anything – your family history, your business history, village history – never put accurate in the title, because you'll regret it.'

By 1986, I'd returned home and back into rural journalism.

By now, Jennifer's search was active again and she was becoming increasingly frustrated by closed doors and lack of information. I thought it was only a matter of time before she would find someone in Carnarvon who remembered her mum. It would be some years, before I'd be in a position to offer too much practical help.

Cupid's arrow was about to strike me too. In 1990, I married an agricultural scientist and farmer Harry Gratte. Jennifer was best woman at the wedding. Harry's best man was his longtime friend Lindsay Horner. When we were first married, Harry and I lived for a few months in Marj's little yellow and white caravan, parked inside our old tin packing shed. This was the caravan Marj and Henry took on their fishing trips up north.

My seemingly indefatigable grandad died that December, just

short of his century. After 99 years and seven months, he was tired. His time on earth had come to an end.

We had started redeveloping the Day property, as well as continuing to work full-time. In the first couple of years, we planted 5600 grape vines and 830 fruit trees, mainly citrus. Windbreak lines of Casuarina trees went in, to line the boundary fences and later, we planted hundreds of eucalypts. Then, of course, there was fruit to pick. Year after year. For decades to come. Life ticked along with the usual disappointments, some highs, a few losses, and then in 1994, our son Joel arrived.

I co-authored a book, kept picking and selling fruit, and in 1997, had a baby daughter, Anna. Jennifer and Geoff along with Lindsay and Marilyn Horner, accepted our invitation to be godparents to our children at their respective christenings. Rural journalism had gone out the window. The travel was just too hard with children and a farm. After the children started school, I began researching their father's line. Following Una Whiteman's example, I tracked back from what we knew, tracing registered births, deaths and marriages, to arrive at Henry James Joseph Gratte, watchmaker and soldier, who seemed likely to be our man.

Although we had a computer by this stage, emails and the internet were yet to come. Research was slow and costly, using snail mail and having to pay for each certificate, some of which would prove to be false leads. Then, Henry James Joseph Gratte threw out a challenge across the centuries, by disappearing off the record books around 1840. It took more years of ad hoc research, doing what I could when I could, sifting through reams of microfiche and noting anything vaguely relevant.

The breakthrough came one morning in the library of the WA

Genealogical Society. We had a birth record for Mary Ann Gratte, daughter of Henry James Joseph Gratte, watchmaker, of Hawkesbury Street, Dover. I'd been trawling through a trade directory, similar to the directories Chris Jakes had shown me back in Cambridge. But this was the 1839 Pigot's Directory of Dover. There was no mention of a watchmaker named Gratte, but Henry Maskens was listed, a watch and clockmaker at 12 Hawkesbury Street. It appeared our man had changed his surname to his mother's birth name, in order to escape the earlier marriage and make a new life.

We contacted descendants of his second family and discovered his new life had been a happy one. They were just as surprised as we had been. They had no idea that their ancestor had a first wife and child. This assumed identity would remain an educated guess until eventually, DNA would set the record straight.

At some point, I was picking grapes with a former policeman friend of ours lending a hand. Picking grapes with someone is a bit like a long bus ride, a rich ground for conversation. Talk turned to family histories and I shared with him a terrible story that had never been written about, so no names will be mentioned here. In another place and at another time, a mother had been unable to pay the rent on the land the family was leasing. She'd locked her eldest daughter, her only surviving daughter and just a teenager, in a room with the landlord and later, a child had been born as a result. I made some throwaway comment about how wrong it was that the pregnant teenager would have been judged by those unaware of the circumstance in which her mother had placed her. 'No-one should judge the girl,' the old copper agreed. 'But no-one has any right to judge that mother either.'

That pulled me up. I had always judged that mother. But then, had I ever been as desperate as she must have been? Had I ever been that hungry? I hadn't lived in her time. Three other daughters had died in infancy, one just a few weeks before the event with the landlord. The mother herself would be dead within three years.

When Marj died in 2007, Jennifer asked Gail and me to help her put together the eulogy. Talk again turned to the vast information gap, so little was known about Marj's childhood. Had she worn her hair in plaits, as Jennifer had done? Someone made the comment, 'Who would have plaited Marj's hair?' It was not that long after this that one of those serendipitous events happened that can turn a situation on its head.

Lindsay and Marilyn Horner's son Chad had started dating Kirsty, an engineer whose mother Verna had family links with Carnarvon. Verna's birth name was Fong, and the Fong and Quan Sing families had been prominent members of the Carnarvon Chinese community. Marilyn had told us that the Fong family had been evacuated from Derby to Fremantle, during World War II. When the war ended, they'd planned to return to their old home town, but got as far as Carnarvon and realised they'd found a new one. Verna and her husband Bill had lived in the town for some years before moving to Perth.

Marilyn also had her own family links with Carnarvon. Two of her Dad's brothers Jim and Charlie had lived there. She knew them to be bush-savvy blokes, who could navigate by the stars.

Family-history tragic Marilyn had been following Jennifer's story. The Horners and the Durrants had come to know each other well through their friendship with us. Whenever Harry and I get together with either or both sets of godparents, two topics of conversation can be guaranteed. The men will gas on about fishing, while we women conduct deep and meaningful discussions about genealogy.

Marilyn has traipsed through cemeteries in remote eastern

Australian settlements, simply to check a few facts. Closer to home, she has researched stories of murder and intrigue. She has the genealogy bug real bad.

By the time Chad and Kirsty married in 2010, Marilyn had already asked Verna if she or any of her extended family remembered the Quan Sings. Had anyone ever mentioned a young girl called Marjorie King who was almost certainly related to the family and knew such a lot about Carnarvon? Yet again, there was the same answer. They knew the Quan Sing family, quite well as it happened, but no-one had heard of Marjorie King. Marilyn asked the same of her uncles and their families. Of course, they knew the Quan Sings, they had the shop by the waterfront, everyone in Carnarvon knew them. But no mention of Marjorie King.

By coincidence, Verna's group of friends included Lily and Nugget's daughter Julie QuanSing-Rowlands. Every year, Julie attended a get-together of former Carnarvon locals, who'd been in her late parents' wide circle of friends. At their next gathering, Verna mentioned Jennifer's quest to Julie and her remark triggered a few memories. Hadn't Julie's mother Lily mentioned a visit from a young woman who believed her mother was Lanky's daughter? And didn't her late uncle Winson mention telephone calls from a young girl in Perth, wanting information about Lanky and a girl called Marjorie King?

Julie's curiosity was piqued and she said she was more than happy to help if she could. The message fed back to Jennifer and me via Verna and Marilyn. Contact with Julie QuanSing-Rowlands was the logical next step. They said Julie was really approachable. She was lovely, just give her a call.

Frustratingly, life then threw another spanner in the chase in the form of 2012. It was a hellish year for both Jennifer and me. My mother went into hospital and Dad died that May and the rest of the year disappeared into a black hole of hospital and aged-care visits, juggled with estate management. Just to keep things interesting, we picked a combined 61 tonnes of Verdelho and Chardonnay that summer and sold oranges, seven days a week, from home, through winter into spring. The children were still at home, so the school run provided some sort of structure to each day.

It was May 2013, before another event happened that would open-up new highways of inquiry. It came in the form of an article in Saturday's *The West Australian*. Even the headline seemed prophetic, 'Students to learn about failure.' Julie QuanSing-Rowlands was quoted in the article and there was a picture. She had a broad smile and looked just as warm and approachable as we'd been told. I picked up the phone to call Jennifer but she'd already seen it.

'We need to pull our finger out,' was all she said.

5

THE QUAN SING CONNECTION

– JD –

When I saw that photograph of Julie QuanSing-Rowlands in Saturday's *The West Australian* in May 2013, I thought, 'OMG, I really need to contact her now.' It was a sign.

Thank God for email because Cheryl and I were both really busy and it was hard to meet up to talk about the best way to approach Julie. Cheryl's Dad had died, and she was sorting all of that. Her Mum was in aged care and she was managing the family property as well as her own kids. There wasn't much time for family history research, particularly, someone else's family history.

Besides, Cheryl and I were still really nervous about making contact with the Quan Sings. Julie's parents hadn't been able to tell me much and nor had her uncles when I'd made contact way back in the Eighties. We were also a bit suspicious that maybe people weren't telling us the whole truth. People of that older generation often avoided talking about subjects they felt uncomfortable with.

By this time, I was fairly confident that Mum had been born outside of marriage. Was that what everyone was hiding from me? It was a long time ago. Surely, these days it wasn't all that much of a scandal, maybe it was the circumstances surrounding Mum's birth. I had so little to go on.

So I really wasn't sure how Julie would respond to a letter from me. Would she even be interested? And if so, would she know anything? Her parents hadn't seemed to.

There were so many questions and doubts. Was Mum full Chinese, or half Chinese? Was the correct spelling of her name Marjory or Marjorie? Such a basic question. But Mum had signed her name Marjory on her marriage certificate in 1948, but later in life, preferred to use Marjorie. That is the spelling I have chosen to stick with for the most part, however, the other form has been used occasionally, too.

That marriage certificate was another puzzle. Although, Mum had told me that she believed her father to be Kinverns (Lanky) Quan Sing, the father is shown as unknown on the document with just a line through the space for the father's rank, profession or occupation.

There is, however, an entry for Mum's mother's name, but this was almost impossible to interpret. On one side, it appears as Annie or Amie Dantau or Dautau or Dantan. On the reverse side, the first name is even more difficult to read and the surname King has been added to the part of the surname starting with D. The only bit that made sense was that Mum had used the surname King because it was the name on that Commonwealth Bank account.

Because three of the Quan Sing brothers had Kin or King or Ken as part of their first names, I'd always assumed Mum's surname King had been directly related to this. And that she'd taken the name King when she came down to Perth from Carnarvon to be educated at Lawley Ladies' College.

We discussed the possibility that Mum may never have known her mother, in which case, she could only have been going by what other people had told her. If there was something the Quan Sing family found uncomfortable talking about like a baby born out of wedlock, would they have even told Mum the truth? Would anyone be willing to tell me the truth? It didn't seem likely from the reactions so far.

One of our email conversation sums up our state of knowledge,

> *Because when you think of it, Marj did spend her first 16 to 20 years in Carnarvon. There must have been some friends. She must have gone to school. There must have been other people who would have remembered the little girl at Quan Sing's store.*

A few days later, I went over to Cheryl's and we drafted a letter to Julie. We wanted to make it fairly general, just asking if she knew of anyone in her family who was interested in family history and telling her that Mum was certainly of Chinese origin and came from Carnarvon. Also, that my interest was genuine. I scanned a couple of pictures of Mum, one as a young woman in a studio portrait where she's wearing a white blouse and a tartan pinafore, and one with the four York kids when we were young. Maybe Julie might notice some family resemblances, something to reassure her that my inquiry was sincere. I didn't want anything from the Quan Sing family, just information.

We also talked about Mrs Burrows, the name that had been mentioned to me by both Winson Quan Sing and Pat Bird. Cheryl had found some old newspaper articles where a woman with the same surname admitted having had an affair while married to her first husband. Later, she had been tried and found guilty, initially of shooting her second husband whose name was Burrows. The second marriage was in 1923 and the couple had lived at a remote mining settlement, somewhere up north. Could Mrs Burrows have been Mum's mother? It was alleged that a woman of that name had a relationship with Lanky and had left Carnarvon, not long before Mum was born. The dots weren't exactly forming a perfect line, but we didn't have much to go on.

Time was ticking on. Mum and many of her friends had either passed away or were nearing the end of their lives. I had nothing to lose by contacting Julie. Maybe she'd be able to put me in contact with someone who knew a bit more.

This is my first letter to Julie.

10 June 2013

Dear Mrs QuanSing-Rowlands,

I was interested to read the recent article in *The West Australian*, as much for your surname as the good work you are doing.... Hence this letter, in the hope you may be able to direct me to a member of the Quan Sing family who is interested and has some knowledge of the family history.

My late mother, Marjory, came from Carnarvon to Perth around the time of World War II. We think she attended Lawley Ladies' College in Mt Lawley before training as a nursing aide at The Mount Hospital where she met her future husband, Henry York. They married and had four children.

Mum was always reluctant to speak of her early life in Carnarvon. It was only towards the end of her life that I was able to learn anything about her past. She was part-Chinese.

Mum said her family name was Quan Sing, and that she spoke Chinese until she was five or six. We believe she was encouraged to change her name to King, when she came to Perth. Her early memories included sitting on back steps hearing the family speak Chinese, a plantation and waterfront shops. She also recalled a small boy called Gary, who was hurt in an explosion. She believed she was closely related to Kinverns Quan Sing, who was known as Lanky.

Mum's date of birth was November 25, 1924, but this was apparently a guess as no record could be found of her birth being registered. She did not ever speak of her mother and we assume she either died young, or had no part in raising Marj.

Years ago I spoke to Mrs Lily Quan Sing, and also Ken and Winson, who could not remember Marj but said she must have been part of the family from the information she remembered. Perhaps she was known by another name in Carnarvon.

My notes from that time also show that I spoke to a person called Pat Bird. She remembered Lanky and said he married late, to a nurse (Pauline) who was a sister at Carnarvon Hospital.

I am sorry if this appears disjointed, but this is what I have to work with so far.

As Marj now has great-grandchildren who resemble her in many ways and may therefore one day be interested in learning more about her history, and theirs, I am hoping to put together some more pieces of the puzzle for them.

It is also a personal quest, as I would like to know more about where my Mum came from.

> I realise that much time has now passed, but would certainly be most grateful if you could put me in contact with any family members or friends who might be able to help.
>
> Kind Regards,
>
> Jennifer Durrant.

Nothing could have prepared me for the warm welcome I was about to receive, first from Julie and her husband Richard Rowlands and later, from the huge Quan Sing family. In our first telephone call, Julie told me that she remembered her mother Lily saying that a lady had come around asking questions about the family, years ago. That lady was me. More recently, she had heard from Marilyn and Lindsay Horner's relative Verna Campbell, at one of the annual gatherings of former Carnarvon people. Someone was still on the hunt for information about Mum. Julie has since provided the backstory to that connection, going back to friendships made years ago in Carnarvon and which have been maintained through the generations since.Verna's parents Daisy and Clem Fong had owned the Drapery in Carnarvon and had been very close friends of Julie's family. Bill Campbell had worked in the Commonwealth Bank and by coincidence, had met Julie, through one of her school friends, who worked at the same bank branch. Verna and Bill had met and then married and moved away from Carnarvon, but met up again with Julie through bank business and also through mutual friends, who had worked in Carnarvon and were also good friends with Julie's parents, Lily and Nugget Quan Sing.

> My Mum would always catch up with Cheng in Perth when they both moved here and we used to take Mum to their place often. Since Mum passed away, we have continued this connection and now regularly go to Terry and Cheng's Boxing Day lunches and Chinese New Year celebrations.

> It was during one of these gatherings that Verna mentioned she had heard about someone wanting to track her family and that years ago, this same person had made contact with my Mum. I don't think Jennifer or Marjorie's names had been mentioned, at this stage.

Julie also told me that Verna's comments prompted a memory of her mother telling her at the time that I had made contact, although she did not mention my name. Julie's mother had said to me that day that what had happened in the past should stay there.

> Mum didn't want to pursue the matter, or be of any help, Julie said. She continued on.
>
> At that time, I felt that Mum was not fair in cutting off the link.
>
> I did ask Mum if she had any contact details and whether she did or not she didn't give them to me, so I couldn't pursue the connection. Also, out of respect for Mum, I am not sure that I would have followed it up.
>
> Then life took over and this meeting faded into the distance until I met up with Verna.
>
> So when Verna mentioned it, I recalled that Mum had actually told me about the meeting just after it happened and I remember saying to Verna that Mum should have been more receptive and tried to help Jennifer in her endeavours.
>
> That's why my initial reaction this time around was to immediately want to help. I felt so sorry and sad that things had been left so long and so late for this connection to be made again.

The story Mum told me about the young boy, Gary, who was hurt in an explosion, was also familiar to Julie. Her older brother Gary had been hurt after playing with a box of matches near a fuel drum. He was about five years old. Julie said the housekeeper had grabbed him and pulled him to safety.

That made me wonder, once I had time to think about it later. Was Mum that housekeeper? Had she pulled the small boy called Gary away from the flames? Is that how Mum knew about the incident in the first place?

Julie said her knowledge of the event was a little sketchy. She was born in 1954 and Gary was thought to have been about five or six when 'the flaming drum event' happened, so it looks like the event happened before Julie was born. So she contacted Gary and asked for his firsthand account.

> As for the incident with the empty petrol drum – well, I think I was about five or six years old – just a little tacker!
>
> As I recall, the empty petrol drum was left under the eave, on the river side of our wonderful home, and I was sitting on top of the drum, singing something like 'Jacky, Jacky, sitting on the wall' when I decided to strike a match and plonk it into the drum. I think Dad had used the drum as a step/leg up to get onto the roof to do some maintenance.
>
> You may or may not know that empty petrol drums contain heaps of petrol fumes, which are very combustible – that is why engines spray a fine vapour/mist into the cylinders, for better combustion.
>
> Well, it went BOOOOM in a big way and hot gases came out the outlet into which I was peering. This of course burnt my entire face – a bit like putting one's face into the steam coming out of a large kettle or pot for minutes!!

It also turned the shape of the drum into an egg shape. Dad later cut it in half lengthwise – it made the best horse feeder bin!

The lady who came to my rescue was Nora Cooyu, who was a robust woman of the Yamaji people, the people of the Gascoyne and Meekatharra region.

George and Norah Cooyu lived in a house Dad had built in the middle of the property, and had a son and daughter….they worked as plantation workers and domestics, helping out with whatever needed to be done.

Norah apparently wrapped me up in her generous body and then wrapped a blanket around me.

Wrapped up in the blanket like this, Mum and Dad then drove me in the truck to hospital where I was bandaged up like an Egyptian mummy. They had to feed me through a straw via a hole in the bandages.

Mum and Dad were very concerned, but apparently I was very cool about my predicament. Mum told me this on many occasions.

Thanks to Norah's quick thinking, there was no permanent damage.

That answered one question. But raised another. Gary would have been five or six around 1949/1950. By that time, Mum was already married to Dad and had Philip. She could not have been anywhere near Carnarvon when 'the flaming drum event' happened. I wondered how had she come to learn of it?

Geoff and I first met Gary and other members of the Quan Sing family at a Chinese New Year celebration that Julie had organised. It wasn't organised specially on my account, but Julie thought it would be a good way to introduce me – and all my questions – to the different lines of the family who would all be in the one place at the one time.

At some point during that night, I got talking to Julie's cousin Wendy Schulze. Wendy's late mother Doris was the daughter of Suithor (Zephyr) who was one of the sisters of Julie's father Nugget. Zephyr was the fourth child, born 1900, then came Lanky, born 1902. Nugget was next in line, born 1904. Technically, therefore, Doris and Julie were first cousins because their parents were sister and brother. This makes Julie and Wendy second cousins.

The significance of that conversation was that I realised Wendy's mother was Doris Schulze, a name I remembered from all those years ago. Dad's sister-in-law, my Auntie Gwen, had told me that Doris Schulze was someone I needed to talk to. Was this the same Doris, I wondered? Was I now sitting, talking to her daughter?

It seemed likely. Auntie Gwen and Uncle Fred had lived and worked in Dalwallinu, and Doris and her husband Oliver had lived and worked in Wubin. But Doris had died in 2005 and Wendy didn't know why Auntie Gwen had encouraged me to make contact with her mother.

I have now seen a wedding portrait of Doris Schulze and can hazard a guess as to why. Doris bears quite a striking resemblance to Mum as a young woman. Doris married in 1952 when she was 23, the same age Mum had been when she and Dad married in 1948. Auntie Gwen would almost certainly have noticed the resemblance and being quite a chatty person, probably asked a few questions. Maybe she'd discovered the Quan Sing connection to Mum years ago. I really felt that another opportunity had been missed. Doris was gone and with her the chance to ask what she knew if anything.

Our next big meeting with the Quan Sing family was early in

2014 at Julie and Richard's house. Julie had put out the call and was expecting several branches of the family to be there. She didn't know if they would be able to tell me any more about Lanky, but said they were bringing along their information about the family. She sounded pretty excited to hear more and wrote that talking to me had for her 'been like taking a trip down memory lane…', adding, 'I look forward to seeing all the photos and any documents you have as well; we have dug out a few bits and pieces too.'

I couldn't wait to meet them and see those bits and pieces. Cheryl came with me, partly, for moral support, but mainly, to write things down. I wasn't sure I'd be thinking clearly enough to take notes.

Julie's cousin Glenis Ayling was at that meeting and later sent me a detailed copy of the Quan Sing family tree. I will briefly try to summarise the main branches of that tree here to better show some of the connections along this journey. This is in the form of a genogram which is intentionally not complete. The names of those present at the Quan Sing gatherings I have attended are included, along with their ancestors, to show how they fit in. Also included are those I either spoke to, or who in some way later proved relevant to the story of my journey to discover Mum's identity.

Therefore, the brothers, sisters, partners and children of the present generation are not shown, except in the case of Julie's husband Richard Rowlands. I think it's important to stick as closely as possible to the story of my journey towards 'finding' Mum.

According to Glenis's records and information from original birth certificates, Yee Chun Quan Sing fathered 13 children. The first two were born in China before he came to Derby. As there is no record of the mother's name, it cannot be assumed to be Kimbly Ah Wing who was the mother of the Australian-born children.

Eleven children were born in Derby, two died and nine survived, two of whom were later taken back to China. According to information on the birth certificates, the youngest child Winson was the only one not to be born at home.

Hence, the abbreviated version of the Quan Sing family tree is included at the end of this chapter.

Present at that magnificent lunch were Julie (daughter of Lily and Kingwell who was known as Nugget) and her husband Richard; Glenis Ayling and her adopted sister Karen Hendrix (daughters of Sideral/ Si Quan Sing and William Harold Ayling); Ann Mayston (daughter of Rita Castledine who was the daughter of Suithor/Zephyr Quan Sing Scott); Ann's cousin Wendy Schulze (daughter of Doris Schulze who was another daughter of Suithor/Zephyr); Robyn West and Kim Hubbard (daughters of Doreen and Kinton (Ken) Quan Sing). Julie's (now late) Auntie Joy was also there – not a blood relative but a very dear friend of the family; Julie had lived next door to Joy when she was at school in Geraldton.

It might be necessary to refer to the genogram and check out those names and connections.

It is fair to say that both Cheryl and I were quite overwhelmed that day.

One of the first pieces of information to come out was that Quan Sing means thousands of successes or many successes. Glenis's research had found that Quan Sing Yee Chun and Quan Sing Yee Lock, who were believed to be brothers, had set sail from Canton and arrived in Western Australia in the late 1880s.

But it was Quan Sing Yee Chun who was of interest to me because he was Lanky's father. Glenis had found a description of Quan Sing Yee Chun as 'a respectable resident and storekeeper of Derby since

1889'. She had also noted that the storekeeper Quan Sing Yee Chun was known as Quan Sing in all business and legal dealings with the government. It was thought that this is why the surname had evolved to be simply Quan Sing. I was starting to feel a bit of information overload.

Then the photographs came out and I couldn't believe there was one small black and white picture of Lanky with his truck, loaded with wool bales. Straightaway, I knew I'd seen that photograph somewhere before. There was also a black and white family portrait, thought to have been taken around 1912 in Derby, of the seven oldest surviving children of Quan Sing Yee Chun and his wife Kimbly Ah Wing. In descending order of age, they were Una, Ena, Zephyr, Lanky, Nugget, Su and Ken. The portrait did not include the four youngest children, two daughters who were taken to China and did not return to Australia, and daughter Sideral and son Winson.

The four girls are wearing immaculate white dresses with ribbons in their hair and the three eldest are each holding an English language book. The youngest daughter, presumably Su, is cradling a doll and Nugget is holding up a small trophy. Julie and Glenis said the books were a sign of the value the parents placed on education which was highly prized. The children were sent to good schools.

I was struck by the likeness between Nugget, who looks to be about eight years old, and my brothers when they were about the same age. Nugget had quite a chunky build, whereas Lanky appeared tall and lean. He reminded me of my nephew when he was a boy. This was the first photograph I'd seen of the person who possibly grew up to be my grandfather.

The subject of Mum's education at Lawley Ladies' College must have come up around this time and we discussed who might have funded it. Julie told me Lanky had been a generous, benevolent person and she could quite believe he may well have paid the school and boarding fees. But she had no evidence or knowledge of this.

Glenis also asked if we had seen the information online about Una's fight with government authorities back in the early 1920s. The article was headed, 'The privilege of employing natives: the Quan Sing affair and Chinese-Aboriginal employment in Western Australia, 1889-1934'.

We had seen it. It did tell us that Una was well educated, capable of running the family business in Derby and determined to stand up to the authorities when she believed she was being discriminated against. So, although it was interesting, we didn't dwell too much on it. We had to avoid distractions and there seemed to be so many.

Una had never married and died in Perth, in 1959, aged 63. The family had formed the impression from conversations with the previous generation that Una had not wanted to have children. As the eldest daughter in such a big family, she had done enough looking after children when she was young. She'd had enough.

Una was very stylish, attractive and confident and had been a real friend and confidante to Julie's mother Lily. Gary described Una as an elegant woman, tall and slim, with an eye for fashion and a talent for dressmaking. She would cut a fine figure at the annual Carnarvon Racing Carnival in one of her own slim-fitting dresses with gloves, handbag and patent leather shoes with heels.

Julie's Dad Nugget was hard working, friendly, artistic and musical. He had worked many jobs including wood and wool carting, shiftwork as a wharfie, as well as working the plantation. He had played many musical instruments and had even played in a band at the Carnarvon Hotel. Well-liked and well-known, he was more of a bohemian than a businessman. He was entertaining company and enjoyed a good joke.

Ken was quieter and a more astute businessman. Well-mannered and refined, he aspired to rise above working class, and moved in the right circles. Sideral, Glenis's mother, was quiet, gentle and easygoing, the sort of person who didn't create a fuss. Glenis and Karen, the baby who had been adopted by Sideral and Bill Ayling, in 1957, have since shared the story of the two adoptions relevant to that line of the family.

And the sadness of a baby, also named Karen, who had lived only three days, having been born with a congenital heart defect. Glenis takes up the story,

> Karen, my wonderful adopted sister, arrived in Derby in my Mum's arms. Karen, her family, and my partner John and I have since met her birth mother Lilian, who was Malaysian Chinese and died some years ago.

But there had been another adoption, much earlier, in 1937, almost 11 years before Glenis was born. And for years, she'd had no knowledge of that event.

> Sideral's firstborn child was Thelma Maureen Quan Sing, born in Melbourne, Victoria, in May 1937, and adopted in January 1938 by Peter Wing Shing, a wholesale fruiterer, and his wife Margaret Young Shing. Her adoptive parents gave Thelma the name Barbara.
>
> The first I knew I had an elder half-sister was years later, when the then University of Western Australia Adoption Counselling Referral Centre contacted me. You could have knocked me over with a feather!

That contact led to Barbara meeting Glenis and other members of her birth family in Perth, where Barbara died some years ago.

The youngest, Winson, who I had spoken to first in 1981 and again in 1986, had been engaged to a friend of Julie's mother, but had ended that relationship and had remained single. He was remembered as something of a loner and careful with money. He'd been in the RAAF in World War II.

Cheryl and I had later looked through Winson's RAAF papers. The enlisting officer had summed him up, as 'a bright lad, neatly attired and well-mannered, exceptionally keen to serve. Should do well on training course'. Winson had applied to join as a trainee wireless mechanic, having given his trade as radio dealer and also later, banana grower. This type of work was familiar to me, as both my brothers had worked as television repair technicians when they were younger.

There were also letters, telegrams and a signed report from the Carnarvon District Medical Officer, from 1945, stating that Kinverns Quan Sing was suffering from severe headaches and had been advised to see a Perth specialist. Winson was required back in Carnarvon to manage the family business and work on the plantation.

Winson's appeal had been rejected by the Office of the Deputy Director General of Manpower, WA, on the grounds that the quota that had recently been granted, for discharge of serving personnel to the rural industry, did not provide for this type of industry. Winson was eventually discharged from the RAAF on 5 February 1946.

I was more interested in the timing of Lanky's illness and his supposed need to see a Perth medical specialist. According to Glenis's notes, it had been reported in the Carnarvon *Northern Times* on 22 March 1946 that Lanky Quan Sing was on a well-earned holiday in Perth.

This was just over a month after Winson had left the RAAF and presumably, was then available to help out managing the family store. So had this given Lanky the opportunity to come down to Perth to seek the medical treatment he needed? He had married nurse Pauline Harcourt not long afterwards. Had they met when he was being treated for those severe headaches, in Perth?

I liked what Julie remembered about Lanky. Mum had told me she believed him to be her father. I was hoping not to be disappointed by what others remembered, but had to be open to any information I might hear. Julie described Lanky as generous, family and community-minded, a person who would help out anyone in any way he could. He loved children and was disappointed when there were no surviving children of his marriage. Hearing that, I had to wonder. Had he ever known about Mum? It is often said that it's the little things that someone does, rather than the big things, that sums up the type of person they really are. Julie described one such incident that said heaps about Lanky's kindness and generosity.

> The parents of my friend, Adele Dawson, always sang his praises, due to their need for an engine to pump water. They couldn't afford to pay for one at the time, and didn't have the money for a down payment … Uncle Lanky gave them the engine and told them not to worry about paying him until they were able to do so.

Despite all this, I still wasn't sure exactly when the family had moved down to Carnarvon from Derby. That would have to wait. Meanwhile, Cheryl was going to do a bit more delving.

Without a birth certificate, I didn't know for sure that Mum had been born in Derby, as it said on her marriage certificate. Other information did not seem to match what I'd been told. I didn't even know if Mum's date of birth was right.

One of the strongest memories of that 2014 lunch is watching the reaction when I brought out my photographs of Mum. There was the wedding photograph, a couple of Mum before she was married and the one taken with the four of us York kids after a trip to the Perth Royal Show.

Everyone thought Mum was stunning. They were handing around the photographs, comparing Mum with various aunties and agreeing that her features were so similar that she must be part of the Quan Sing family.

One of the big questions they kept asking amongst themselves was, 'Is she full Chinese? Or part Chinese?' In the car, on the way home, Cheryl and I were both a bit bewildered. But we were certain about one thing. 'They're just as confused as we are.'

I had no doubt after that lunch that the Quan Sing family had accepted me. Everyone was perfectly willing to talk and so keen to help. They were all so open with me that I no longer thought Mum was some sort of secret they wanted hidden. The truth seemed to be that they simply had not heard of her.

I had gained some sort of certainty that Mum had a family connection to the Quan Sings and I felt a strong connection with Julie, but I didn't really have any new information to lead the search forward. I still wasn't even sure Lanky was Mum's father. It could be that one of his brothers or sisters was Mum's parent.

Una was a possibility, she may not have wanted to have children but stranger things have happened. What if she had become pregnant and hadn't wanted to raise a child, if some other member of the family had raised Mum? Most puzzling of all was that no-one at that lunch had ever heard of Mum. Yet from what she told me, she must have been in Carnarvon when the older Quan Sings were there. The people at that gathering all agreed that Mum must have been there, because she knew so many little details about the family. Details that could only be known by someone inside the loop. I felt more than ever that I was going around in circles.

Julie and I stayed in touch and we caught up a few times at family events, but the next major development on the Quan Sing front happened after I did a DNA test. This was in October 2015. Cheryl had been continuing to go through records and wasn't getting anywhere. She gave me the test as an early 60th birthday present. Two years early, to be exact. She said she couldn't stand to wait another two years.

I wasn't interested in finding out any more about my Dad's line. So much was already known about the Yorks and much of it had been written down. Mum's family history was such a blank page. At least, a DNA test should show whether or not I had Asian DNA, and how much. If any matches happened to pop up that would give me more information, then that would be a bonus.

The test was quite simple and perfectly painless. The results came in just before Christmas. They showed I was 62 per cent European, from Europe West and Ireland. This fitted with what I knew about Dad's family being from England and Ireland. There were also quite a few familiar names from my York line among the matches.

That first estimate also put my Asia East ethnicity at 19 to 23 per cent. This made sense if Mum was half Chinese, then I would be about one quarter. At least it had answered the question about whether or not Mum was full or part-Chinese.

Some Pacific Islander DNA had also shown up, with an estimated 11 to 15 per cent, next to Melanesia. I wasn't really sure what this meant, but guessed it must have had something to do with the Quan Sing line, as the family had migrated from China to the Kimberley.

The most exciting result was that I had a match with a W.D. Schulze and couldn't wait to tell Julie. On December 19, 2015, I sent the following email to Julie and Richard,

> ... Recently, I had a DNA test ... to find out whether there was a China connection. The results came back showing my DNA is 30% Europe West and 26% Ireland (which makes sense on my Dad's side) and 21% East Asia (which includes China) and 15% Pacific Islander.
>
> This was good news to me as an indicator of Mum's Chinese heritage. But there was something else!
>
> It also linked my results to others likely to be related. One of the closest was a W.D. Schulze, also with Asia East in the DNA. The result said with 'extremely high confidence' that we are likely to be second or third cousins ... I was wondering therefore whether or not this W.D. Schulze is likely to be Wendy, the.....Quan Sing descendant, who I met at your place?

W.D. Schulze did indeed turn out to be Doris Schulze's daughter, Wendy! The amount of shared DNA means there's a good probability we are second cousins, or the equivalent. This fits with Lanky (or one of his siblings) being my grandparent. It also lets us rule out Wendy's grandmother (Zephyr) as possibly being Mum's mother, not that we had seriously considered her a contender. But if that had been the case, then Wendy and I should show a closer relationship. Julie is closer up the line to Lanky than is Wendy. Julie's father Nugget was one of Lanky's siblings, whereas, in Wendy's case, it was her grandmother Zephyr. I started to wonder if Julie would agree to taking a DNA test.

It was late in 2017, before I finally went ahead and ordered a test for Julie and I planned to give it to her the next time we met for Chinese New Year. If she felt uncomfortable or unwilling to do it, that would be no problem. I'd pass it on to someone else who might be interested. Having a DNA test had become quite popular. But in her usual enthusiastic style, Julie was more than keen to help. She did the test early in 2018 and emailed through her results.

> I have just received the results of my DNA and it seems I am almost pure! 89 per cent Asia East, 11 per cent Polynesia.

My updated results had also come in, showing that Julie and I were first to second cousins. At this time, Julie was my closest match. She had even pipped some of the York cousins who I knew to be descended from Dad's brothers and sisters. I was definitely quite a bit Quan Sing.

Julie told us she hadn't explored all the data in detail at that point and suggested we get together with Cheryl. So, we organised a lunch date for the following weekend. Julie and Richard were planning to head off overseas and Geoff and I had booked a 10-day break in Hong Kong and Singapore for the end of the month. We met on the day before we flew out.

Julie seemed amused and even a little bit miffed that her test result didn't show she was 100 per cent Asia East. We assumed her 11 per cent Polynesia result probably had some connection with my 11 per cent Melanesia result, both were included under the heading for the Pacific Islander region. (Some of the regional terminology has since changed, but this is what we had to work with, back then.)

It was another great lunch and I really enjoyed hearing more about the Quan Sing store in Carnarvon. I knew from some of the information that had been gathered that it had been down by the waterfront on Olivia Terrace.

On The Heritage Council of WA database, it is described as having sat between a corrugated iron building that housed the Quan Sing's three-tonne Chevy truck and surplus stores and a delivery bay and stock storage area. After the death of Mrs Quan Sing (Kimbly Ah Wing) Senior, in 1934, Lanky had taken over the running of the store with help from brothers Ken and Winson.

I wondered whether the shop had steps? Would this have been where Mum sat, listening to the men talking Chinese? The shop was on the waterfront. Was it along this stretch of beach that the shark had bitten Mum on the knee? Winson bought the store after Lanky's death in 1953. The database describes 'a vibrant local general store, with curios from bygone years, which had intrigued its customers'. But it all went downhill, after Wesfarmers moved into the town in 1951, two years before Lanky's death. When Winson was in hospital, in 1992, children set fire to the old store. Later that year, Winson passed away. What was left of the store was eventually demolished. Not even the sausage tree that had been planted by the Quan Sings remains.

It was brilliant having scientific proof that Julie and I were genetically connected. Our shared DNA fitted the pattern that would be expected, if one of Mum's parents had been Julie's uncle Lanky. But it fitted the possibility of another sibling, like Una, just as well. We could rule out Julie's Dad Nugget, because our match was not close enough for that.

In the weeks prior to the DNA celebration lunch, Cheryl and I had shared dim sum with a big group of the Quan Sing family at Chen's Kitchen, in Wembley. As we were leaving, we mentioned that we planned to drive over to the Chinese section at Karrakatta Cemetery and try to find Una's grave. We'd already checked the location, and printed off a map. The Quan Sings, there that day, said to be sure to look out for the big tree and we'd find Una's grave right near it.

It was a hot March afternoon, in 2018, with temperatures into the low thirties and the grave wasn't exactly jumping out at us, despite the map and the directions. We knew the grave was in the Chinese section BA and thought we were in the right place but could see no sign of it, nor the big tree.

We must have spent over an hour wandering aimlessly around. We ended up walking in a big circle through the heat and dust. We were just about to give up and drive home when I realised we were almost back to where we'd started and there, in front of me, was Una's grave.

To be honest, by this stage I was feeling really flat. In spite of everything that had been found out, I was really no closer to finding out about Mum's early life than I'd been back in 1981. I'd stumbled across Una's grave, but really had no idea whether she was my great-aunt, or my grandmother. The grave was not far from the edge of the path. We looked around but could see no sign of the big tree that was supposedly right near it.

Then we noticed the big heap of sawdust.

The tree had been cut down.

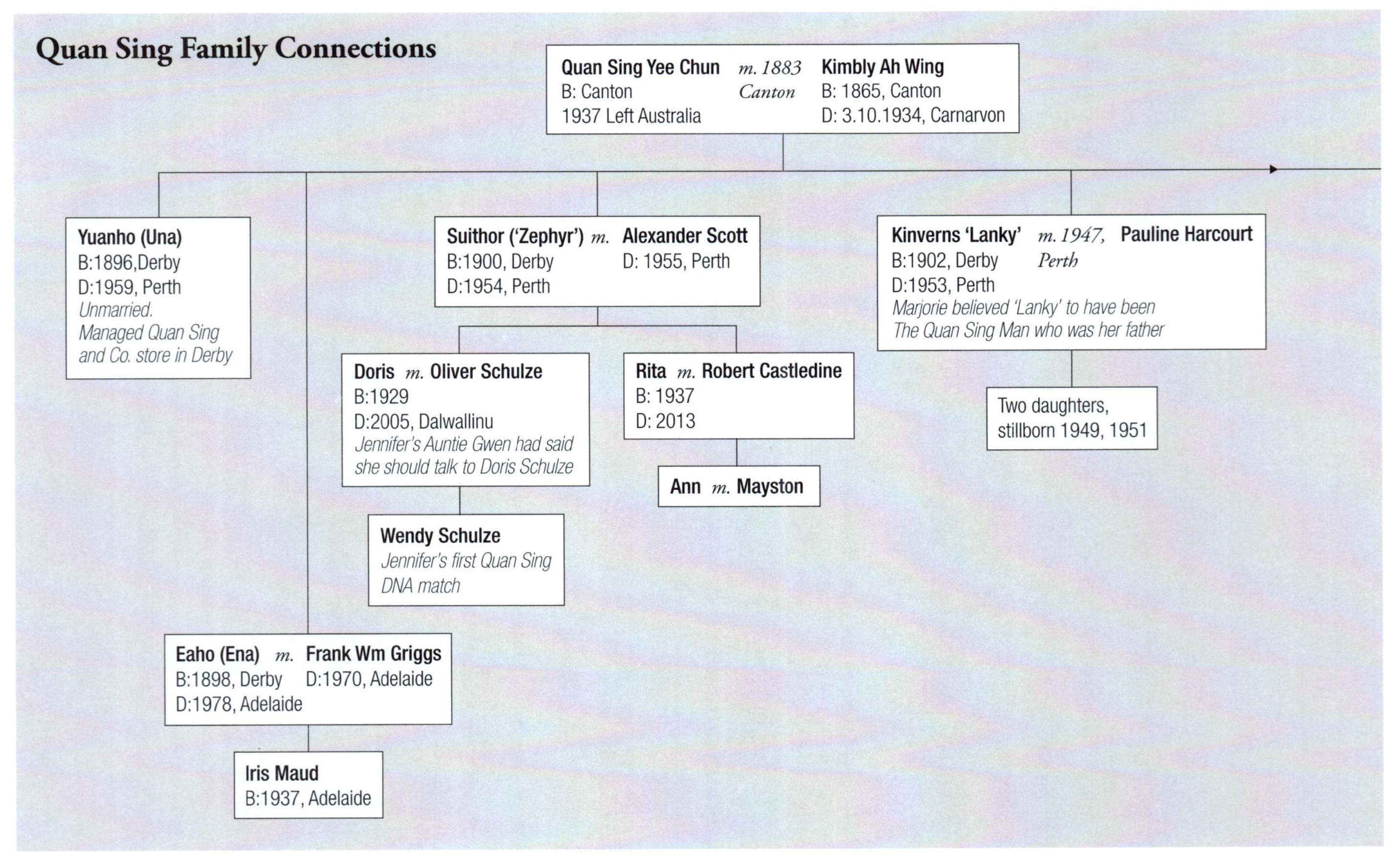
Quan Sing Family Connections
Quan Sing Yee Chun m. 1883 Canton Kimbly Ah Wing
B: Canton
1937 Left Australia
B: 1865, Canton
D: 3.10.1934, Carnarvon
Yuanho (Una)
B:1896,Derby
D:1959, Perth
Unmarried.
Managed Quan Sing and Co. store in Derby
Suithor ('Zephyr') m. Alexander Scott
B:1900, Derby
D:1954, Perth
D: 1955, Perth
Kinverns 'Lanky' m. 1947, Perth Pauline Harcourt
B:1902, Derby
D:1953, Perth
Marjorie believed 'Lanky' to have been The Quan Sing Man who was her father
Doris m. Oliver Schulze
B:1929
D:2005, Dalwallinu
Jennifer's Auntie Gwen had said she should talk to Doris Schulze
Rita m. Robert Castledine
B: 1937
D: 2013
Two daughters, stillborn 1949, 1951
Ann m. Mayston
Wendy Schulze
Jennifer's first Quan Sing DNA match
Eaho (Ena) m. Frank Wm Griggs
B:1898, Derby
D:1978, Adelaide
D:1970, Adelaide
Iris Maud
B:1937, Adelaide

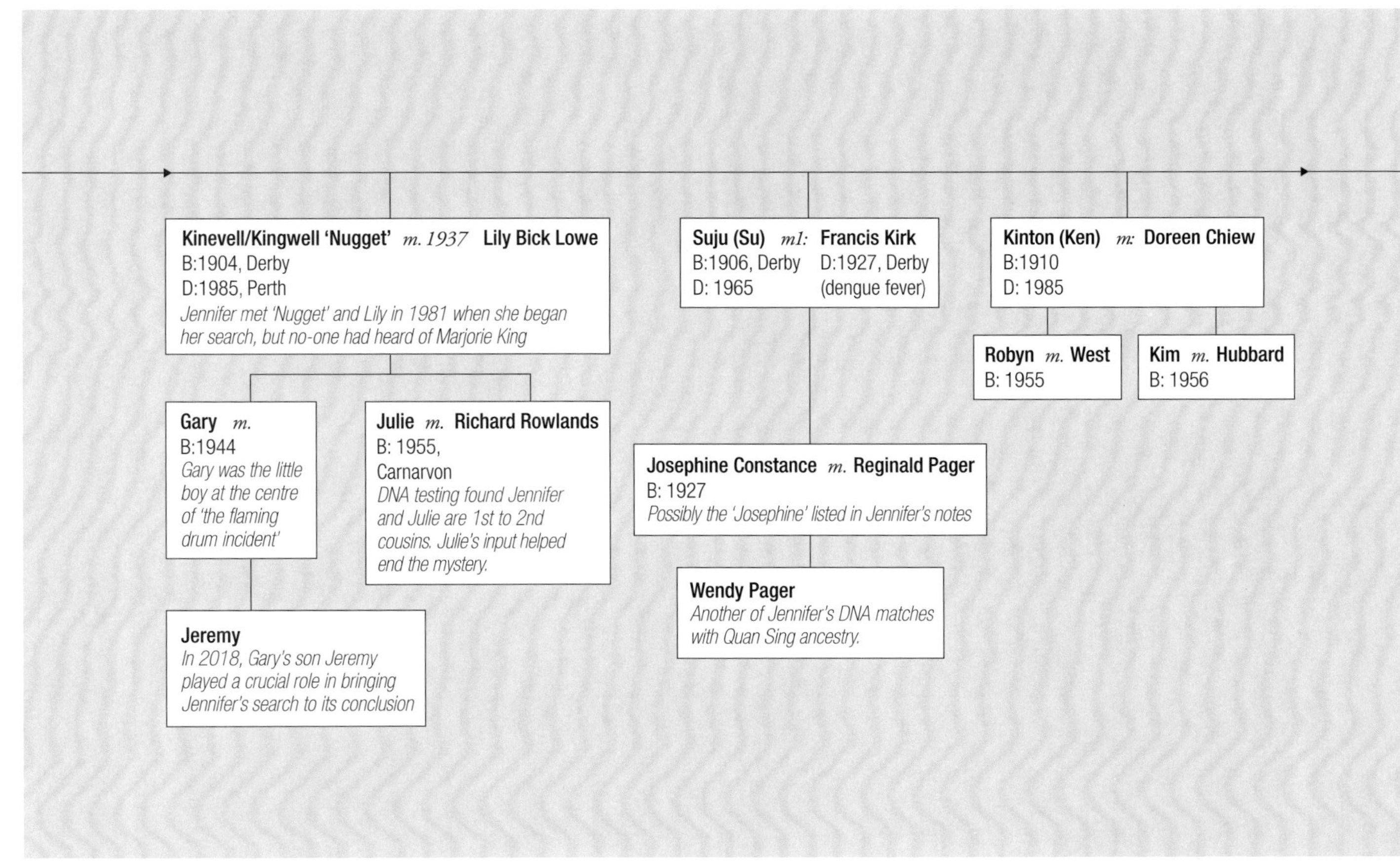

Kinevell/Kingwell 'Nugget' m. 1937 Lily Bick Lowe
B:1904, Derby
D:1985, Perth
Jennifer met 'Nugget' and Lily in 1981 when she began her search, but no-one had heard of Marjorie King
Gary m.
B:1944
Gary was the little boy at the centre of 'the flaming drum incident'
Julie m. Richard Rowlands
B: 1955,
Carnarvon
DNA testing found Jennifer and Julie are 1st to 2nd cousins. Julie's input helped end the mystery.
Jeremy
In 2018, Gary's son Jeremy played a crucial role in bringing Jennifer's search to its conclusion
Suju (Su) m1: Francis Kirk
B:1906, Derby D:1927, Derby
D: 1965 (dengue fever)
Josephine Constance m. Reginald Pager
B: 1927
Possibly the 'Josephine' listed in Jennifer's notes
Wendy Pager
Another of Jennifer's DNA matches with Quan Sing ancestry.
Kinton (Ken) m: Doreen Chiew
B:1910
D: 1985
Robyn m. West
B: 1955
Kim m. Hubbard
B: 1956

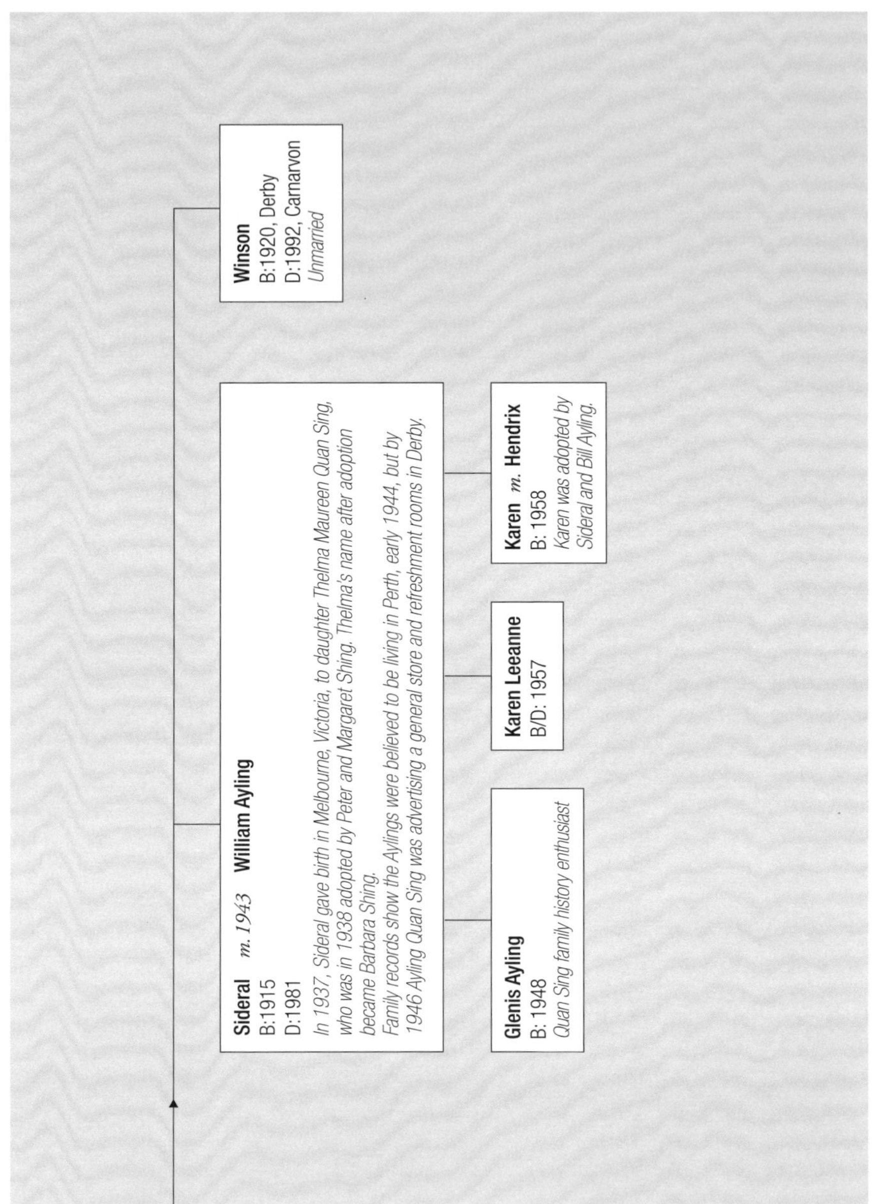

This incomplete tree diagram is included only to show the connections that were relevant to Jennifer's search. Therefore, omissions are intentional.

6

RED HERRINGS, HARD FACTS

– CR –

My mother kept a daily diary from 1 January 1969 until 11 February 2012. Mention of Marj is constant through that span of observations, recorded in neat, cursive script. Around all the daily egg tallies, annual bales of hay cut, the minutiae that back then were threads in the fabric of Swan Valley family life, Marj is a frequent visitor, often bringing with her armloads of vegetables or 'a lovely double sponge'.

As the visits grew less frequent, due to increased distance and reduced mobility, cards, letters and telephone calls maintained the link, right up until Marj's death on 9 July 2007.

Mum's 1994 diary for March 19 says that Marj went with my parents to the Regal Theatre in Subiaco to see *Don't Dress for Dinner*. The trio later had tea together at a fish shop in Midland. Then, on June 16 the same year, there's this,

> Marj rang, her parents used to live in Carnarvon, had a shop. Mother died when she was 10 years old. Dad died 1954.

This diary entry was discovered in February 2016. It was during a time in my life, when I was sorting a lot of family stuff and the diaries had proved a useful resource when I needed to check the date of a significant event. Trawling through them was, however, both tedious and emotionally gruelling. This find, however, was pure gold. Marj's own words, so faithfully recorded, in Mum's neat handwriting.

By this time, we knew that Lanky had died in 1953, not 1954. His sudden death, in Perth, had been reported in *The West Australian,* the following day on August 28. He was described as a well-known Carnarvon businessman who'd conducted a general store at Carnarvon for 25 years. He'd also served a term as a member of the Carnarvon Municipal Council. *The Northern Times* (Carnarvon), the following week, had acknowledged the 'friendly natured, well-known and respected citizen' in a front-page tribute, headed 'Popular Carnarvon Businessman Passes On'. Many memories of this deceased gentleman will linger in the town and among friends on plantations. He had been a grower for the past 18 months where kindly service was always extended to his neighbours.

The diary entry stated 'Dad died 1954', not 1953. But, in the scheme of things, we could allow for that small margin of error. Mum may even have recorded the year incorrectly, when she wrote up her diary that night. Dad had planted 92 brown onions before going to a 'luncheon' in South Perth. Mum had 'cleaned out the fowl pen and pullet pen', had a visit from Bob up the road, with mandarins and oranges, then I'd called in and shared sandwiches on the patio. I was six months pregnant, at this point, with the first of our two children.

We also knew that Lanky's mother Kimbly Quan Sing had died in 1934, the month before Marj would indeed have turned ten. *The*

Northern Times (Carnarvon), on October 10, announced with regret that Mrs Quan Sing had died on October 3, after a short illness. Among the more than seventy mourners listed were nuns from the Presentation Convent. Later that month, the same newspaper reported that Winson Quan Sing was among the Presentation Convent School students who had been successful in the University examination for theory of music. Winson was then 14.

The entry in Mum's diary only posed more questions. Had Marj genuinely believed Lanky to be her father and had she believed that her grandmother Kimbly was her mother? The year of Kimbly's birth is not known with certainty. Glenis Ayling says there is a question mark over the date and place of her birth, as different dates appear in different documents.

According to the birth records of the Quan Sing children born in Derby, Kimbly was 52 when Winson was born. Marj was born over four years later. It was a bit of a stretch, even for us, to seriously consider that Kimbly had given birth to Marj when she was 56. Not impossible, of course, but not likely. Besides, Winson had told Jennifer he had no recollection of Marj. And Winson was there at the convent passing his music theory examination.

We then turned our attention to other potential mothers, first among the Quan Sing daughters, instead. How old were they and where were they in 1924? The younger girls we dismissed quickly, on age alone. Which left Yuanho (Una), Eaho (Ena), Suithor (Zephyr) and Suju (Su) to consider.

Then there were the brothers. Could one of them have fathered the child that was Marj and given her over to Kimbly and Lanky to raise? Again we could rule out the younger boys, but this was all getting complicated. DNA testing would later rule out Zephyr and Nugget.

Jennifer was a match to their descendants, but not a close enough match for either to have been Marj's parent.

Una was our first line of inquiry. She was the eldest, born in 1896, and had never married. Hadn't Marj mentioned an Auntie Una, just called Auntie? It wouldn't be the first family where a child had assumed his or her biological mother to be an aunt.

Information on the public record paints a picture of Una as intelligent, independent and feisty. Like Jennifer, she seemed the sort of person not afraid to call a spade a spade. A particularly well-documented case that came to be known as 'The Quan Sing Affair', describes her stance against authority amidst the racial landscape in Derby around 1920.

The 1925 electoral roll for Derby lists Yuanho Quan Sing as manager of Quan Sing and Company. Interestingly, her sex is listed as M for male. Was this a simple typographical error or was it intentional? Was Una thumbing her nose at the paternalistic time, in which she found herself. The same M is listed again on the Derby roll in 1931. By 1936, she is listed in the Gascoyne as Quan Sing, Yuanno (sic), Carnarvon, domestic F.

The family believed from what older family members had said that Una had never wanted children. But what if Una had become pregnant and her mother and brother had raised the child? Could that child have been Marj? Certainly not an impossibility. It's a common enough scenario in many families. But it still didn't explain why Marj seemed so invisible to so many. She just wasn't on the radar. Una Quan Sing was 63 when she died in Perth, in 1959. She was buried in the Chinese Area at Karrakatta Cemetery.

Next we cast our net a little wider. The Burrows rumour had been niggling away since the mid-Eighties, when Lanky's alleged affair with a mysterious Mrs Burrows had come to light. The Burrows had supposedly left town around 1923 and two sources had believed Mrs Burrows to be pregnant. And Mr Burrows was not happy. Had that Mrs Burrows subsequently delivered a part Chinese baby, it was not beyond the realms of possibility that the child would have been returned to be raised by the father's family. Could that baby have been Marj?

Then, something straight out of left field. In 1937, Perth newspapers reported that a Mrs Burrows was to stand trial in the Perth Supreme Court for the wilful murder of her husband. It was not the first time this Mrs Burrows had been in the news. In 1921, the *Daily News* had reported that her former husband had been a granted a divorce, on the grounds of his wife's adultery with some man unknown. A female child had been born in February 1921, as a result of that affair.

With so much margin for error surrounding the actual date of Marj's birth and the timing of the alleged affair between Lanky and Mrs Burrows, this child had to be considered a possibility. Or another child, from another affair? Remote possibilities but not ones to ignore either.

The retrial produced more evidence that Mrs Burrows had been living and working in the north-west, for approximately 10 years after their marriage, which she stated was on 24 January 1924. The WA Registry gives the year of marriage as 1923.

She told of working on her husband's gold mine at Peak Hill, which is about a nine-hour drive inland from Carnarvon. This information, coupled with the black and white photograph of Lanky's truck loaded with wool bales, posed more questions.

How far inland did Lanky travel, delivering produce in his truck? Was he taking fresh produce inland to the station country and bringing back wool from the sheep on those stations? Could this have been how he'd met Mrs Burrows when she and her husband were working the mine at Peak Hill? Was it even the same Mrs Burrows?

So many questions, for which the answers would have to wait.

I wasted such a lot of time investigating Mrs Burrows. Just as false starts are a curse to a sprinter, red herrings like this are the bane of the family historian. They lure us in, only to lead us astray and waste valuable time. Then again, hidden amongst all those remote clues might be the compass that will point the way home. Ignore the hunch, the seemingly irrelevant detail, at your peril.

The journey to find the real Marjorie King was no exception. It started with her name.

When scrolling through WA Registry Indexes for births in the years around 1924, which surname did we search? King? Sing, or Singh? Quan, or Kwan? Chun? Or something else? In the end, it didn't matter. After searching each possibility, there appeared to be no records in the database that were even a remote match.

The correct spelling of Marj's first name also presented a conundrum. Jennifer has chosen to go with the spelling Marjorie. It was the spelling she seemed to prefer, later in her life. A letter, dated 6 May 1984, written by Marj when I was living in Wales, is signed, 'love from all our family, from Marjorie and Henry York'.

Yet Jennifer has official documents where her Mum signed her name as Marjory King. Even in researching this, we sometimes found ourselves using Marjory and have therefore included that spelling where it was used at that time.

One of the official documents is a copy of her parents' marriage certificate from 1948. A logical starting point, one might assume.

But it too presented puzzles. Marj had always claimed that her father was Kinverns (Lanky) Quan Sing. She'd been consistent in this belief. So why on the marriage certificate does it state 'father not known'?

Her mother's name is stated. That was significant because we'd each independently formed the impression that Marj's mother had died when she was young. We both had cases in our families where babies had been cared for by others after their mothers died in childbirth.

The mother's name was difficult to read but appeared to be Annie Dantau King and elsewhere, the abbreviated Annie Dantau. Dantau was our best guess. The handwriting was so hard to decipher … it may have been Dantan, Dautau, Dautan or even a corruption of Quan. The D and a were positioned, such that if that third letter was u, then Quan was a distinct possibility. And Quan King did not seem a million miles away from Quan Sing. Jennifer always believed that with so many of the Quan Sing males having first names starting with King or Kin or Ken, it made sense that Marj might have adopted the surname King when she'd come from Carnarvon to Perth.

Back to the online indexes, I checked the various forms of Dantan for a birth registered in the years around 1924. Nothing. Another piece of evidence, dating from the King York marriage in 1948, was the image of Marj and the mystery gentleman who had escorted her into the church. Among the suspects in our line-up were Betty Lund's father Ernest Lund and Mrs Ulrich's husband Hubert Ulrich.

Searching Ernest Alexander Lund (1890 to 1955) online led to a military record that tells us he was a driver during World War I. Aged 24 years and six months, at enlistment, he stood 5 ft 10 ½ ins tall, weighed 11 stone 6 pounds, had blue eyes, a fair complexion and fair hair.

That description does not rule out Ernest Lund as the man who escorted Marj to the church on her wedding day. However, despite searching various sites and attempting to contact lines of the family in Australia and New Zealand, I have yet to find anyone able to positively identify him as Lund.

We do have a result for Hubert (Bert) Ulrich. A great-niece returned our call for help and was happy to supply some photographs of her great-uncle, as a young man and in army uniform when he served in the Australian Imperial Force (AIF). We could agree that Bert Ulrich was highly unlikely. His World War I military record stated his height as 5 ft 7 ½ ins, and our man looked taller. The case remains open.

Lawley Ladies' College seemed a bright hope. We knew Marj had been there, because she had told Jennifer about it. And she'd had a passbook for a bank account in Mt Lawley. On Friday, 7 June 2013, I'd saved a cutting from an online chat forum claiming 'the mystery of the Lawley Ladies' College has finally been solved'.

Efforts to find any information from the Department of Education had proved fruitless, but a reader of the online forum had responded to say it was a very private school in Mt Lawley run by a Miss Sharp. The writer went on to say Miss Sharp's mother, known as Grandma Sharp, had lived in a two-storey house just down from the school and was cared for by another Miss Sharp. The latter was known as Miss 'China' Sharp, having been a missionary in China. Those colourful names were a help when trying to track down the Sharps. Grandma Sharp turned out to be Ada Matilda Sharp who made news in 1971, when she died aged in her 110th year. This had earned her the title of Australia's oldest woman. Daughter Mabel Ross Sharp had made even bigger news in 1923, when she and fellow missionary to China Mary Darroch, were kidnapped by bandits and carried off as hostages into the mountains of the Honan Province.

The West Australian, of Saturday, 29 September 1923, reported an update from Mabel Sharp's mother, providing some insight into the character of both. 'She is a brave girl', said her mother proudly,

> ... and we have never had one word of complaint from her since she has been in China...Just about this time last year the Chinese bandits carried off Mrs Soderstrom, a missionary, and her daughter, and Mr Ledgard. He escaped and the women were held to ransom, but released.
>
> My daughter would be wearing only light Chinese clothing, and I fear she may suffer cold and hardship in the hills. They will probably only give them straw to lie on, and already they seem to have destroyed all the missionaries' property. Miss Darroch, my daughter's companion, is over 60 years old, and my daughter would never desert her, even if she had the chance to escape.

Over two weeks later, the same paper published an unconfirmed report that troops had defeated the bandit chief Fan the Terrible, after a hard three days of battle and rescued the missionaries.

When I relayed this fascinating story to Jennifer, she became pretty animated. Like she used to get before a school running race. It was just a small scrap of information, but it got her lights flashing. 'That's who used to visit Mum – the two Miss Sharps – they were the ones who drove the big, dark car!' Well, that was one box ticked and yet more questions posed. If Marj's former school principal and her sister, a former missionary to China, thought enough of her to maintain contact all those years after her marriage, then Lawley Ladies' College was certainly worth a closer look. Nor could the China connection be ignored, given Marj's connection to the Quan Sing family. An advertisement in *The West Australian,* dated 11 January 1936, describes a select college for day and resident pupils, preparing them for all examinations, including University, Junior and Leaving, Civil Service, Nursing and Commonwealth Typists. As well as Business Preparation, it offered a special two-year course for girls, including general educational subjects, business preparation, speech training and dressmaking, claiming 'this course will enable a girl to be self-supporting'.

In 1936, Marj would turn 12. Was this when she would have started making those regular flights to Perth from Carnarvon, to attend what sounded like a finishing school, to prepare her to make her way in life? Or had her Perth education begun when she was even younger?

A report in *The West Australian,* dated Monday, 6 January 1930, tells us the college was established in 1929 with thirty-six students including twelve boarders.

Given the longevity of Grandma Sharp, I was curious to see how long the Miss Sharps had lived. The Metropolitan Cemeteries Board's website states that Rosalie Ross Sharp had died in 1985, at the age of 92. Her sister Mabel Ross 'China' Sharp, had lived until she was 99, passing away in 1990. The location of the place she was living at the time of her death was shown as Bassendean.

In the years leading up to 1990, and for lots of years since, Jennifer and Geoff were living, not a million miles from that Perth suburb. Jennifer used to do her weekly grocery shop, on a Thursday night, at the Bassendean Coles.

When the opportunity for DNA testing became available, one hope was that there would be a direct descendant of one of Marj's parents who would take the test and provide a close match with Jennifer.

We knew that Lanky Quan Sing had married late in his life, in 1947, and the family believed his wife was nurse Pauline Harcourt. Sadly, there were no living children of that marriage. His death certificate states he was the father of two unnamed females (deceased). His own sudden and unexpected death was the subject of a standard coronial investigation that found the cause of death to have been a ruptured aorta. The death record for an unnamed stillborn Quan Sing female infant, born at home to the couple in Olivia Terrace, Carnarvon, on 22 September 1949, gives the cause of death as the congenital birth defect, anencephaly. A second stillborn daughter, born on 13 August 1951, had not survived the consequences of pregnancy toxaemia. It is not known what happened to Lanky's widow, registered nurse and midwife Sister Pauline, after his death, but it appears she did not stay long in Carnarvon. The *West Australian Government Gazette* of 12 May 1958, lists a nurse Pauline Harcourt as working at the district hospital in Port Hedland. It seems likely she reverted to the name Harcourt. The one death record I have been able to find for a Pauline Harcourt was registered in Carlton, Victoria, in 1960, for a person who had died at the age of 48.

Carnarvon remained the focus of the search. Marj had given Jennifer so much information about the town. I kept hoping to find someone who had lived there at the same time Marj must have been there, but time was running out. Then early in 2014, on an ABC North West WA website, I found a 2010 interview with a man called Cyril Smith, who has since passed away. He was described as 'a real Gascoyne institution'. He was born in 1924, the same year as Marj. Supposedly, assuming the date of her birth we were working with was correct.

Cyril had written a book called *Camels to Cappuccino – the journey of a boy and his town*. He described the book as an important historical record of the development of Carnarvon and the characters that had shaped it. I had to find this man and talk to him. So I tracked him down and made the cold call to Cyril and his wife Fay. They were both very interested and keen to provide any information that might help. Cyril told me that when he was a fourteen-year-old, he'd worked for Nugget Quan Sing on his plantation.

The names I mentioned were familiar to them. They even remembered Pauline as having been deeply affected by the loss of children. But Cyril did not remember Marj. They suggested that I send any information I might have in an email to them, to give them a chance to have a bit of a think and ask around. Their response arrived on Sunday, 23 February 2014. This was around the time of that first big Quan Sing lunch at Julie and Richard's house. Scanning the email, I could see they'd gone to some effort to find out what they could. But the result was the same. 'So far we have not been able to get any positive feedback on Marjorie … ' the email began. Their train of thought led them to eliminate some of the Quan Sing siblings, as we had done and they did not have any ideas about the name King either.

> The surname King is a complete mystery, in this case. If there had been a marriage I am sure it could be discovered. The most memorable families in Cyril's time were Quan Sing, Chon Wee, the Fong family came later from further north.
>
> Marjorie's memory of waterfront shops would have been before the river was diverted from coming through the town …

That was another clue. Something else to follow up. Fay, who mentioned then that her second name was Marjorie and the same spelling, said she would remain alert for any possible lead towards the mystery of Marjorie.

The email went on to the now bulging heap of potential leads and dead ends. By this stage, I was starting to experience something of a crisis of confidence. When I'd offered to lend a hand, I'd assumed Jennifer must have missed something. I gave it six months, max, to crack. How hard could this thing be? Quite hard, I was now discovering, with growing dismay.

Despite all those years I'd spent searching archives, trade directories, birth, death and marriage records and talking to people across the world, to unravel a few of our own family's secrets, where Marjorie King was concerned, I'd found out diddly squat.

And this was in my own backyard, Marjorie had never left Australia. She hadn't even had a passport. During her travelling phase, after Henry died, there had been some talk of a trip to New Zealand. But, without a birth certificate, that all became too hard and in the end, she'd decided to thoroughly explore Australia, instead.

The first Quan Sing lunch did little to boost my confidence. The lunch was fantastic, such a friendly bunch, and Julie's spread was superb. What troubled me was the growing realisation that the assembled family, who were all so genuine in their efforts to help, appeared completely ignorant about Marj's existence and were as confused as we were about her ethnicity.

At the next lunch date, in 2018, we had the DNA results to celebrate, but so little else. It was like Marj had not existed, until she'd met and married Henry York.

When Jennifer said she had more or less accepted that she would never find out the story of her mother's life when she was young, I felt dreadful. I'd dropped the baton. There always remained the faint hope that a new DNA match could turn up and provide some direction. That's the thing with a DNA test, it keeps ticking away in the background, delivering updates.

We agreed that Sister Una Florence Ulrich must have known the answer to, at least, part of the puzzle. Talk often came back to Mrs Ulrich. She had maintained contact with Marj all her life. But Mrs Ulrich had been dead since 1985. She had lived out her life in Queensland and had no children we could ask.

7

THE GOLDEN WATTLE

– JD –

Every spring, when we lived on our small farm at West Swan, the bush around our place would come alive with wildflowers. Right out the back and on the old Caversham Airfield, and on the unmade road reserve to the south, were golden wattles, kangaroo paws, smokey bush, even orchids. The reserve was called York Street after our family. Today, this street is part of a Bush Forever Site. Endangered Carnaby's Cockatoos and vulnerable Forest Red-Tail Black Cockatoos feed on gumnuts on the marri trees that are there.

Back then, on the farm itself, the ritual of killing, plucking and dressing the poultry often involved the whole family, especially when Mum made her famous chicken soup. Dad would fill the copper in the laundry and light a fire in the fire box underneath it to heat the water, before catching and humanely killing the chosen chook. It was our job to pluck off all the feathers, even the pin feathers, after the chook had been given a good dunking in the boiling water. I can still smell wet feathers and see us standing by the copper, plucking over the old cement troughs.

Usually we'd do one or two chooks at a time, but sometimes, up to six, as there were a lot of mouths to feed. Nothing was wasted. Even the crop was cleaned out, washed and cooked. Mum would gut the chook and everything, absolutely everything, except the feathers, went into her soup. Giblets, chicken livers, the strings of unformed eggs, even the chicken feet. The nails would be removed and the outer layer of skin peeled off the legs and in they'd go to the soup, along with the onions, carrots, potatoes or any vegetables we had handy. Once I was older and started going out to restaurants with friends, I started to notice that most Chinese restaurants had chicken feet on the menu. I hadn't known it was a typical Asian dish and thought that was a sign of just how Asian Mum was, the way she used to cook with chicken feet. The flesh on those feet in her soup had a gelatinous texture when it was cooked. Once they were sucked and licked clean, there was so little left that what was left reminded me of toothpicks.

I never order chicken feet when we go out to a Chinese restaurant. I had my fill of those when I was younger. But I am always reminded of Mum's special chicken soup, whenever I see chicken feet on a restaurant menu.

Another example of Mum's habit of using everything, of never letting anything go to waste, was that she would eat the roe from the fish she'd caught. I don't remember Dad doing this, but it was something Mum always did. I don't remember any of us kids arguing for a share of the fish roe either, but to Mum it was a delicacy, something she savoured. It was special.

Mum was an excellent cook and her bible in the kitchen, particularly in the early years, was *The Golden Wattle Cookery Book*. Fruit mince pies, lots of fruit cakes, ginger nuts and all sorts of biscuits, puddings like lemon pudding, sago snow and lemon snow and bottled fruit and pickles. You name it, she made it. Not that I loved everything. I hated brawn, which she sometimes made with kangaroo meat, loathed white stew and brains made me gag.

One of Mum's stand-outs was her sponge cake, which she made using her Mixmaster. She had one of those heavy, old white Mixmasters, from the Fifties. I think the coming of the Mixmaster was a big thing for a lot of Mum's generation. They saved women having to use all that elbow grease. I remember the egg whites had to be beaten, until they were really light and fluffy, so the sponge would be sure to rise. Mum's recipe used just one goose egg, but her sponges rose so high that one half would be the size of a double sponge. They were enormous!

Mum used to cater for family celebrations like 21st birthdays. She made all her own clothes and for significant events, she sometimes made herself something really special in the style of the *cheongsam*. This was another sign of her Chinese heritage and some of that must have rubbed off on me. Just before I turned 21, I went to Singapore and Bali with my friend Stephanie. When we were in Singapore, I had a *cheongsam* custom made and loved it.

Mum didn't use her old *Golden Wattle Cookery Book* so much as the years went on. I guess, she had made some of those dishes so often that she knew them by heart.

After Mum died in 2007, I kept that old cookbook, even though it was falling apart. Quite a few pages were missing and it had lost its back cover. But I kept it because it was so old. And because it had been Mum's. I must have put it in a safe place. Like so many things that are put in a safe place, I didn't see it for years. In fact, I hadn't thought much about it. An old photograph album of mine had also gone missing and I'd been hunting for it, off and on, for about four years, without any luck. Then in December 2017, I started a big clean up. Geoff and I had decided we'd put our house on the market and were aiming to list it with a real estate agent in January 2018. That meant we'd have to have a photographer come in and take photographs of the exterior and the interior for the real estate website. I had decided to do the styling myself rather than bring in a stylist, which would have cost us an arm and a leg. But first, I had to declutter. We'd been in that house since 16 December 1985, almost bang-on 32 years, so there was quite a bit of decluttering to do.

For starters, I had around 3000 books to get rid of. Most of them were in our front room where Geoff had installed some magnificent jarrah bookshelves he'd built all along one wall.

The front room was our formal lounge, the first room that any prospective buyers would set their eyes on. I wanted to create a good first impression and that meant moving on a good chunk of those books. I was going the full bottle on minimalism and clean lines, colour co-ordination, you name it, I was taking the whole 'styling' challenge very seriously. It had become my pet subject.

It was on Sunday, 10 December, that my friends came over. They'd offered to give me a hand to sort the books and move, what we could, out to a local charity shop. So all this sorting and chatting was going on and then, someone pulled out a couple of books from Geoff's shelves and out fell the photograph album that I'd been searching for all that time. And with it, out toppled two old cookbooks including Mum's *Golden Wattle Cookery Book* right onto the carpet. They'd all been in the same safe place all those years.

I bent down to pick up *The Golden Wattle Cookery Book* and started looking through it. It was pretty easy to tell the recipes that Mum had used most often from the condition of the pages. The favourites were on the pages that were most worn or were stained with ingredients, used all those years ago, back at our little place at West Swan. Quite a few of the pages were missing completely, along with the back cover.

But the front cover was still in place. I flipped it open and inside was an inscription. I didn't remember having seen it before, but I immediately recognised the handwriting. It was the same handwriting that I had come to recognise when I'd collected the mail from the big letterbox, down the front of our old place in West Swan where we all grew up. The distinctive writing of Una F. Ulrich, Mum's old friend from Queensland, who had shared my room back in 1975 when she came over to Perth by coach, for Dawn and Jim's wedding.

That night, I emailed Cheryl and I told her how two old cookbooks and the missing photo album had turned up. Then, I wrote,

> In one of the books, it had, 'To Marjory in her 15th year, 1940 –
> With every good wish for your future. From Sister. U.F. Ulrich.'

Well, there you go!

There was a smudge under the signature, but I didn't take much notice of that. There were so many stains and smears through the book, it may not even have registered with me. Besides, I had a house to style.

On the 32nd anniversary of us moving into our house, I messaged Cheryl with a photograph of our styled main bedroom. The For Sale sign went up on our front lawn on 26 January 2018. The full set of 18 photographs went up on the sales agent's website. I was pleased with how the property presented. All the sweat and tears about styling had been worth it. It was such a relief.

I was about to learn that more sweat and tears were ahead. Keeping a home looking immaculate, when you're juggling a full-time job with 'open home' days and inspections by interested buyers and stickybeaks, is no picnic. I barely had time to think about much at all, let alone think about Mrs Ulrich. I was too busy thinking about whether or not the place needed a quick going over with the vacuum cleaner, before I went off to work.

But I was still no closer to finding out the truth about Mum. I felt incredibly flat.

Geoff and I were flying out on holiday soon and I was looking forward to getting away. I needed the break. I was shattered. Done. I had reached the end of the line.

8

THE ULRICH FILES

– CR –

Una F. Ulrich had been a person of interest in Jennifer's search right from the start. Sister Ulrich, as she was often called long after she'd retired from nursing, had corresponded regularly with Marj until the former's death in Queensland in 1985. She had known Marj before her 1948 marriage to Henry York. So she must have had some knowledge of Marj's early life, more than Jennifer had, at least.

Jennifer remembered Mrs Ulrich as a very religious person. Her parting gift after her 1975 visit had been a copy of the Bible, with written thanks to Jennifer accompanying an inscription she'd written inside. Jennifer had formed the impression that her Mum had either worked for or been cared for by Mrs Ulrich when she was younger.

This had prompted me to download a copy of 'ROADS: Records of Adoptions – an index of locations and access to adoption records', early in 2016. It was a document, developed to help make historical records more accessible to people seeking information about adoption. ROADS listed contacts for the various state government and non-government agencies, such as church missions and care facilities, as well as hospitals including Carnarvon and Derby.

Although we had no proof of Mrs Ulrich having adopted Marj, Jennifer wondered if her Mum had perhaps been her ward and therefore, if there would be information held on a file somewhere. Another long shot but the nearest we'd been able to get.

Harry's Uncle Stan who is well-versed in local history, having been awarded the Medal of the Order of Australia in 2009 for his service to the community through the Geraldton Historical Society, learned of Jennifer's quest for information. He had strongly suggested that we needed to target finding Marj's file, assuming such a file existed.

A year later, in April 2017, we got as far as downloading an application for adoption information, but the form was never filled out. There remained too many uncertainties about the when, where and who, for either of us to be confident about providing information that was accurate and meaningful.

We were still not completely sure about the name Marjorie King. Was it Marj's name from birth or had she taken it when she'd left Carnarvon to come to Perth to Lawley Ladies' College? No record had been found of her birth and nor could we state with any certainty the identity of her father, even though Marj had told Jennifer she believed him to be Lanky Quan Sing and we knew there was a strong genetic Quan Sing connection.

Marj's mother's identity also remained a complete mystery. We also knew from the Quan Sings that homebirths were the norm at that time. How much time could we afford to waste chasing up what might well turn out to be yet more dead ends?

Inevitably, perhaps, the forms were filed away in the too hard basket along with all the other dead ends and red herrings. The too hard basket was starting to fill up. This research was all being done on the fly, in spare time around the edges of fulfilling but busy, sometimes frantic and often frustrating work and family demands. My mother had died in September 2017. In the years preceding that event and the months that stretched into years afterwards, there was not a lot of spare time.

Then Marj's old *Golden Wattle Cookery Book* had turned up quite unexpectedly in the weeks before we'd hit our lowest point. Jennifer had accepted that she would never find out answers to questions she'd been chasing since 1981 and I felt about as useful in the genealogy stakes as a second-hand Leyland P76.

So when Jennifer and Geoff headed overseas on 22 April 2018, I was determined to give the Mrs Ulrich hunt one last crack. The logical starting reference was a scrapbook with any snippets of information relevant to Marj. At this point, Una F. Ulrich and her husband Hubert (Bert) occupied seven pages. There was enough to build-up the skeleton of a time line and hopefully get some direction about the point where Marj had intersected that line.

Maybe this chronological approach would help shine some light on places or past events to examine more closely, in order to move the search forward.

The racist language, used in some of the newspaper articles, quoted in the following pages, may offend some readers. It is reproduced here because it was the language used at that time.

Family history sites indicated Una Florence Austin was born on 24 April 1899, in Queensland, the eldest in a family that would grow to four children. By 1922, she is on the electoral roll as a nurse, working at the Children's Hospital, Herston. The 1925 and 1926 electoral rolls show Una Austin as living at home with her mother Ellen and sister Ina in the electoral sub-division of Buranda. Still listed as a nurse, this would have put her close to both Brisbane Children's Hospital and the Diamantina Hospital for Chronic Diseases.

When Una Austin and Hubert Ulrich married on Friday, 14 September 1932, at St John's Cathedral, Brisbane, the event was announced in the family notices section of *The Brisbane Courier*, the following Thursday.

> ULRICH-AUSTIN – At St John's Cathedral, on September 14, by the Rev. W. Hoog, Hubert, eldest Son of Mrs C. Ulrich, Fremantle, W.A., to Una Florence, eldest Daughter of Mr and Mrs W.J.H. Austin, Brighton, late of Boonah.

Although it is stated that Hubert is the eldest son, it would soon come to light that eldest surviving son would have been more accurate. A reminder that even the most simple of facts when probed can reveal layers of truth. A more detailed account of the wedding was published in *The Northern Standard* (Darwin) on Tuesday, 18 October. The minister officiating was the bride's cousin but in this account his surname was 'Hood' not 'Hoog'. We know now that 'Hoog' was more likely correct. There was another story in *The Brisbane Courier*, earlier in 1932, when the Rev. W.H. Hoog was presented with a gold Swan fountain pen and pencil by parishioners of St Albans, in the Brisbane suburb of Wilston. This detail may seem picky and a sidestep to the search for Marj but it was nonetheless another reminder never to assume something to be fact, even when published in a supposedly credible source. Small details, but Chris Jakes and Una Whiteman might appreciate them.

The Northern Standard report also offered a few clues, amongst the descriptions of morocain and lupins, typical of that era.

> Una F. Austin, lately Matron of Boulia Hospital, was married to Hubert Ulrich, late of Darwin and Broome, W.A.
>
> The bride wore a simple hand embroidered white satin frock and carried a bouquet. Her veil was lent by her sister, Mrs A. Ward. She was attended by Miss M. Colthup, cousin, who wore a graceful frock of green morocain with a beach visca hat and carried a bouquet of pale pink lupins.
>
> The bride's mother entertained the party in the Canberra after the ceremony. Mr George Katterns, who is well known in Darwin, acted as best man.

A report in *The Cloncurry Advocate*, 20 August 1932, tells us that Matron Austin had planned to leave Boulia on August 18. At a meeting of the Boulia Hospital Committee, it was resolved to write to Miss Austin expressing appreciation of her services whilst Matron at the hospital. It is not yet known when she began working as a nurse there, as her name appears on the 1932 electoral roll as Matron, Boulia Hospital, but not on the 1931 roll.

The Boulia Shire Council site today describes a vast western Queensland shire of 61,635 square kilometres. There are two towns; Urandangi to the north and Boulia on the banks of the Burke River. Boulia is a long way from anywhere, 536 km from Longreach, 383 km from Birdsville, 366 km from Winton and 328 km from Cloncurry.

The Brisbane Courier of 11 October 1932, provides an idea of the degree of isolation and therefore, the extent of responsibility carried by medical professionals in such a remote outpost back then.

And harsh economic times meant the hospital was struggling.

> By reason of the serious falling off in subscriptions and the consequent reduction in Government subsidy during the past few years, the finances of the Boulia Hospital have been causing grave concern....(it) is 200 miles distant from any other hospital, and considering that it serves an area of some 25,000 square miles, it would be a calamity to the residents as well as to the travelling public if it had to be closed.

Reports in other local newspapers, around this time, paint a grim picture of a harsh and unforgiving landscape in a country of extremes. Drought, soaking rains, a lost station hand found dead from dehydration not far from a river, serious injuries that, by virtue of distance from help, did not get medical attention for days.

The challenge of attracting trained nurses to Boulia had been noted back in December 1928, when *The Townsville Daily Bulletin* published a report of the Hospital Committee meeting. The meeting had supported a move to write to Mr A.J. Powell, Medical Agent, Brisbane, asking if the services of an A.T. N. A-trained (Australasian Trained Nurses' Association) nurse were available 'and to advise promptly'. The great difficulty of getting any trained nurse to go out as far as Boulia was noted, ending with 'they all preferred waiting about the large coastal towns'.

Una Austin, by this time around thirty and with several years of nursing experience behind her, had put up her hand for this. At the time of their marriage, Una was 33 and Hubert a few short weeks away from 42. The marriage posed another question, how on earth did this couple meet? Although both had amassed some considerable life experience by 1932, from what's been found on the public record, so far they appear to have been working in different parts of

Australia. And in Hubert Ulrich's case, his life had been interrupted by five years offshore, caught up in the bloody battlefields of World War I.

His military service record tells us he joined the A.I.F at Guildford, Western Australia, on 28 October 1914, when he was aged 23 years and 11 months. This was just weeks after 10 August, the date recruiting offices had opened in Australia. Hubert Ulrich's Regimental Number was 17. The military record lists his trade or calling at enlistment as pearler. This matches the occupation, listed against his name on the 1916 electoral roll, when his contact address is Broome. Presumably, therefore, he was working as a pearler in the weeks or months before enlisting.

Also, according to his military record, Hubert had spent five years as an apprentice carpenter (to J.M. Ferguson) and had accrued three years' service in Naval Rescue in Fremantle. The occupation of carpenter is also listed against his name on the 1949 and 1954 voter lists later in his life, when he had returned to live in Fremantle. Fair complexioned and with fair hair and blue eyes, he stood 5 ft 7 ½" tall, weighed 150 pounds and his chest measurement was 36 to 39 inches, at the time of enlistment. Hubert Ulrich served with the 10th Light Horse, initially as a trooper/signaller and within a year, had been promoted to Corporal.

Just over two months earlier, on 6 August, his older brother Sergeant Frank Ulrich had been killed in action at Lone Pine. *The Sunday Times* of 10 October had published a photograph of the older brother with the caption, 'Sgt Frank Ulrich, 11th Battalion, killed on his first day in the trenches'.

Three days before Hubert Ulrich's arrival at Gallipoli, Perth's *Western Mail* had carried a full-page tribute, under the banner The

Roll of Honour, with images of 25 men, either killed or wounded at Gallipoli. Frank Ulrich's portrait sits to the immediate left of Private W. Simpson, 'The Man With The Donkey'. Frank Ulrich's military record tells us he too had been working as a pearler in Broome, which was where he'd joined up in February 1915.

Hubert Ulrich survived World War I, and voter lists in 1922 and 1925 show him living in Broome and again working as a pearler. By 1931, he is working as a pearler in Darwin, marginally closer to Una in Queensland but not much.

We pick up Hubert Ulrich again in June 1933, after his marriage, when he writes an impassioned report in *The Telegraph*, Brisbane, about poaching of pearl, trochus and turtle shell in northern Australian waters by Japanese fishers. He writes about the need for a fast and seaworthy craft, commanded by a pearling master or ex-master, to patrol these waters.

The Telegraph describes the author as, 'Mr H. Ulrich, of Brisbane, who except for the years he was on war service has been for a great number of years master of pearling fleets from Broome round to Thursday Island.' If Hubert was hoping to be offered command of such a patrol craft, it apparently did not eventuate.

For, in March 1934, there are two separate newspaper articles, indicating that Una, at least, is working as matron of the hospital at Mt Garnet, now a former copper, tin and lead mining town, described on tourist sites as the link between the tablelands and Cairns to the north and the Gulf of Carpentaria and Darwin to the west. The Visitor Centre website also notes there were 14 tobacco farms in the area in the early 1930s.

Under 'Mt Garnet Notes' in *The Northern Herald* of 17 March, mention is made of Matron Ulrich 'who is kept busy with hospital patients, has found time to form a sort of junior league among the young girls, some of the objects being classes for first aid and elementary nursing'.

The following Friday, in *The Cairns Post,* there is a public notice, thanking 'Matron Ulrich, of the Mt Garnet Hospital....for kindness shown during our sad bereavement ...'

Conditions at the hospital were primitive, according to a letter to the editor, published in the 4 October 1933 copy of *The Cairns Post,* where Queensland MLA for The Tableland and Minister for Works Harry Bruce describes an inspection that he had made, at the request of the Australian Labor Party and the hospital committee, 'The building was in such a dilapidated condition that to my mind and the mind of the district foreman of Works ...it was not advisable to effect any further repairs.' A nearby property had been identified for purchase, as it was more suitable to be used as a hospital, and the present building was to be removed, he went on.

But a suitable new hospital building was not up and running by 12 June 1934, when Harry Bruce writes again to the editor, stating he had finalised the property purchase and authorised the necessary alterations to be effected without delay by day labour to convert the building into a cottage hospital. By December, the 'very essential repairs, painting and structural alterations' are yet to be completed.

Reports indicate the minister visited Mt Garnet to officially open the new first aid and maternity hospital in May 1935 but by then, Una F. Ulrich was about to move on. *The Cairns Post* tells us on 4 July 1935, that a new matron had arrived to take charge.

Voter lists for 1936 put Una (nurse) and Hubert (miner) further north at Cassowary Creek, near the tin-mining centre Herberton, in the Atherton Tablelands.

The Cairns Post, of 9 December 1936, lists a Mr and Mrs H. Ulrich, among passengers on board *The Canberra*, en route from Cairns to Melbourne. Presumably, they carried on to Western Australia, for on the 1937 electoral roll, we find Una (nurse) and Hubert (clerk) back on Ulrich family home turf at View Terrace in East Fremantle.

From an article in *The West Australian,* on 25 March 1937, we can plot some of the couple's movements after leaving Fremantle.

> Mr and Mrs H. Ulrich, the latter also being a fully trained nurse and former hospital matron, will take up duty at Moore River Native Hospital at the beginning of April, and will later proceed to the North to take over one of the native hospitals there.

This once again gave rise to the thought, albeit briefly, would a part-Asian child like Marj have been considered a child of colour? Might she have been removed from Carnarvon, and taken to Moore River? That thought had first surfaced earlier, back when reading the much-documented battle with authorities had by another Una – Una Quan Sing in 'The privilege of employing natives; the Quan Sing affair and Chinese-Aboriginal employment in Western Australia, 1889 – 1934.'

Although Australian born and educated, she had been discriminated against on the grounds that her parents were Chinese and in the eyes of the law, she was therefore deemed to be Asiatic.

Other newspaper articles made mention of 'half-caste children brought from places as far distant as Carnarvon' to missions and reserves in the far north. ('Blacks in the North – The Chances of the Half-Caste', *Western Mail*, 9 August 1934) Could Marj, being part Chinese, have been taken from the Quan Sings in Carnarvon to one of these missions or reserves?

Could that be where she had first met Mrs Ulrich? It seemed unlikely. It didn't fit at all with the little detail Marj had told Jennifer about the Quan Sing family and Carnarvon. If there was an intersection point to be found, I thought it was far more likely to be some sort of hospital or nursing post around Carnarvon.

Tracking Una F. Ulrich through the paper trail highlighted the reality that the window of opportunity for the meeting was relatively narrow. She had spent the bulk of her working life in remote areas of Queensland.

Her time in Western Australia was relatively short, from 1937 until late 1941, and again around 1949.

Not long before leaving Perth in 1941, she had written a terse and pithy letter to the editor of *The Daily News*, Perth, published on 1 October.

Headed 'Kimberley Natives', she'd written,

> In *The Daily News* of 24 September you have an article entitled 'A.I.F. Recruits Meet Hostile Natives.' To me the article looks like cheap publicity for a picturesque individual whose imagination may be as picturesque as his appearance. I have never regarded it as cricket to attack anyone behind his back and in my opinion natives are equally entitled to this consideration. I have known natives from all the tribes in the Kimberleys, there are some very fine men and women among them. – UNA F. ULRICH (A.T.N.A.), Perth.

In 1943, Una (home duties) is listed on the electoral roll as living at a hilltop address, 5 km from the Brisbane CBD. But she was only passing through. *The Longreach Leader* of 24 December, reports that Sister Ulrich, Sister in charge of the Barcaldine Maternal and Child Welfare Clinic and who also visits Longreach and Aramac, had submitted suggestions to the local council to try to improve the health service.

> Sister Ulrich stated she has applied to be released from her position before Christmas for private reasons, but, as there was no one available to take her place and the clinics would have to close down for a time she put her own affairs to one side and offered to remain until a relief sister could be found.

Barcaldine is 67 km from Aramac and 107 km from Longreach. Part of the problem, in 1943, was that the clinic sister's mode of transport to these outlying sub-centres was the train.

Sister Ulrich remained at the clinic, until April 1944, when she advised Longreach Shire Council that the centre and sub-centres would close indefinitely due to lack of staff. Council responded with a letter to the Premier and the Minister for Health and Home Affairs, and the local MP, as reported in *The Central Queensland Herald,* on Thursday, 27 April.

> Community astounded to hear baby clinic closing here on 20th inst. Would you kindly endeavour to have this essential service continued for benefit of mothers and babies in this town.

The Carnamah Historical Society and Museum site, listing nurses working in Western Australia 1919-1949, shows Una employed as a general nurse at 55 Lincoln Street, Perth, in 1949. This was the birth year of Marj and Henry York's first baby Philip and provides evidence that Mrs Ulrich was in Perth at that time.

The Perth hospital where Una found work in 1949 was the Alexandra Home in Highgate Hill. An article in *The Western Mail,* dated 30 September 1926, describes it as a home established to shelter, support and educate young unmarried mothers.

It would also appear that, at some point in the 1940s, the Ulrichs separated. By 1949, Hubert is based in Fremantle working as a carpenter and Una is about to return to Queensland, where she would continue working to deliver health care to remote communities.

Queensland Country Life, 28 May 1953, informs us that Matron Una F. Ulrich was 'doing a great job....serving humanity in the Gulf', in her more than two years in charge of Burketown District Hospital.

> Matron Ulrich was in Cairns when she heard that Burketown Hospital had been closed for some months. Always interested in the outback, she became doubly interested when she learned that many of her patients would be aborigines, and she went.
>
> Matron faces drought, heat, fire and flood and any emergency with indomitable courage. She does the doctoring (the Flying Doctor makes his routine call monthly), the nursing, cooking and breadmaking with as much zeal as she makes curtains, sheets and baby clothes.

Some idea of the conditions at Burketown can be had from *The Cloncurry Advocate* that, on 8 August 1952, had published a report by Consolidated Fishing Industries research director Dr John Bell.

> Dr Bell states that water amenities are deplorable, for after the rain water tanks become dry, supplies have to be carted in drums from a bore in the main street … to the hospital, and stored in tanks until used. In front of the hospital is a largely eroded area filled with town rubbish of empty tins etc – including night soil tins. Only 100 feet from the hospital, this dump is extremely unhygienic, to say the least…in wet weather, the hospital grounds become a quagmire, forcing the Matron to wear rubber knee boots when walking between the buildings.

> Attempts have been made to improve the conditions in the accommodation of the natives, by the Matron, who is also compelled often, to do post-natal washing, without proper facilities, in the open. The mortuary is literally an oven.

It went on to list the Matron's duties: cooking, cleaning, dental extractions, dispensing and treatment of patients, both surgical and otherwise.

Una remained matron at Burketown until at least 1958, according to the electoral roll, but the 1963 roll rated two listings, one as Matron at St Luke's Hospital, Yarrabah and at an address in the Brisbane suburb of Annerley, occupation listed as nurse.

The 1968 roll finds Una back in Brisbane and from 1972 to 1980, her address is given as Bruce Highway, Kulangoor, where she was laid to rest in the Garden Lawn Cemetery, on 7 January 1985. On the voter lists right up until 1980, she had maintained her occupation as nurse.

Una F. Ulrich, presents a far different person from the straight-laced, myopic, frail, elderly person that Jennifer remembered from 1975. Her solo coach journey from Queensland to Perth may not have been as daunting to her as we had assumed.

Had Jennifer and I known this much about Una F. Ulrich's backstory, five or ten years ago, it is tempting to think it might have influenced our approach in the search to find Marj. We have since had the chance to consider this. And the truth is, a change of tack was never going to be likely when we had so much anecdotal evidence linking Marj with the Quan Sing family and Carnarvon. All of it from such reliable sources as Marj herself and my own mother's diary. And where would we have started.

It was the night of ANZAC Day, 2018, just a few weeks after Marj's cookery book had turned up, with Una's signature inside the cover and three days after Jennifer and Geoff had headed overseas. Time as usual was short. I sat down at the computer to give the Mrs Ulrich hunt one last crack.

I must have been playing around with the choice of keywords to type in to search, then I tried Mr and Mrs Ulrich. Immediately, up popped the reference code for two of their personal staff files held by our own State Records Office (SRO). The SRO is a huge resource. Their records come from more than 1300 individual state and local government agencies, many of which are now defunct.

That defunct is wherein lies its appeal and usefulness. In 2006 and again in 2016, I had become involved in two separate local causes requiring accurate historical information, to present to those prepared to take up the fight. For the record, one battle was with a state Labor government, the second with a state Liberal government. My opinion, partly as a result of this, is that we must always be on watch, no matter, who is in power.

One consequence of the 2016 campaign was setting up the Saving Our Swan Valley Facebook page. Saving Our Swan Valley was also an online archive, saving stories and images about the people and places that are part of Swan Valley history. People and places, whose stories were at risk of disappearing, unless we kept and shared them. One result of managing that page was that Leanne Old, from Collie, contributed. My grandmother Vera had been friends with Leanne's grandmother Dorrie, when they were growing up together at Middle Swan. Our family albums held beautiful studio portraits of Dorrie's family. But as many were not labelled, it was impossible to work out who they were, let alone what their lives had held. What were their stories? Leanne was able to fill many of those gaps and flesh out the bones of a family of musicians and educators who delivered much to the Swan Valley and the state. Later, Leanne would play a key role in helping to solve one of the sub-plots in the search for Marjorie King.

So I already knew what a wonderful repository of records is held by the SRO. One file covered the Ulrich's time as officer-in-charge and nurse at the Hospital, Moore River Native Settlement. The second, their time working in the same roles at Derby Native Hospital. The second file hardly seemed worth pursuing. By this time, we knew the Quan Sing family had left Derby and relocated to Carnarvon long before 1937, which is when the Ulrichs had arrived in WA.

Glenis Ayling had found a 1923 customs declaration by Quan Sing Yee Chun, stating he was the father of Kinton (Ken), born 1910, at present residing in Carnarvon.

Also the tribute to Lanky Quan Sing in *The Northern Times* of 3 September 1953 had stated that he had come to Carnarvon when he was 14 to work for his uncle and had taken over the store in 1929. If correct, that meant that Lanky, born in 1902, had come to Carnarvon around 1916.

Nonetheless, if I was going to order one file, it seemed opportune to take a look at the other one too. The two manila folders were ready the next morning when I called at the collection desk. The Derby file, in particular, looked like it would present quite a work-out. The correspondence started with a letter of application for a position in Wyndham, written by Hubert Ulrich, in October 1936.

I settled in at one of the work stations and began a fairly vigorous session of speed reading and speed writing. At some point during the day, one of the records office archivists drew my attention to another work station where a camera was set up for scanning, specifically to help users to capture images of the information they wished to study. All users had to supply was their own thumb drive.

The next day, I returned and scanned 67 pages, using this method. The details would have to wait, until Jennifer got back, when we had more time to digest the contents. In the midst of all this, a name, written in Una F. Ulrich's all too familiar handwriting, caught my attention. Remembering the advice about finding the file, I asked at the help desk whether this particular file might exist.

'You need the Personal Names Index,' the archivist told me. 'It's being used at the moment.'

He indicated another SRO user, a woman of about my age, quietly working away at one of the desks in the corner. Fighting back an urge to rugby tackle a contemporary, I listened, as the archivist suggested I go away and have a cup of tea. The other user would be finished with the index soon, he assured me and pointed to the shelf at the back of the room where the index would be waiting when I got back.

Over that cup of tea, I had time to consider what the index might contain. I read that it was compiled by the then Aboriginal Affairs Planning Authority and contains references to over 5000 people of Aboriginal descent, who are referred to in departmental files held by the State Records Office and to personal history cards, held by what is now the Department of Aboriginal Affairs.

The file was where I'd been told it would be when I pushed open the door and returned to the State Records Office. I sat down and opened it, then read down the alphabetic list to the names starting with K. And there, against a familiar name, was a number.

9

THE MARJORIE KING FILE

– JD –

Geoff and I got back from Hong Kong and Singapore late on Tuesday, 1 May 2018. We'd had a great time away and we'd both needed it. Before we left, nothing had been going right. Our house had been on the market for four months and although there had been quite a bit of interest and heaps of inspections, there had been no offers. One potential buyer had even wanted to rip out the beautiful bookshelves Geoff had made from century-old jarrah. Let's just say, I was a bit tired!

Then there was the hunt for Mum. All of that seemed to have stalled.

When we got back, we hit the deck running. The next day, I made the 70-km round trip to collect our Jack Russell Pepper from kennels in Canning Vale. There was the food shopping to do, all the washing and the house to clean and keep styled for more prospective buyers. The real estate agent knew she could bring people through at relatively short notice, which meant the house always had to be tidy. It was almost like we'd never been away.

In the middle of all this, I had a text message from Cheryl, 'Hi Jennifer. When would you like to meet?' This was on our first day back. I suggested the following Saturday, 5 May, 'No home open, so what time would suit you? All I have to do is have a photo taken for my driver's licence.' Cheryl asked me to bring the cookbook Mrs Ulrich had given Mum. She said she wanted to take a photograph of it. That was interesting but I didn't think that much of it. But I was a lot more interested, when the day before we were due to meet, she messaged me again. 'Can you pls bring that bw pic of Mrs U with Marj, the cook book and some form of id like driver's licence or passport for scanning. ☺'.

This was on Friday morning, 4 May. Straightaway, I thought, 'Omigod, something has happened!' I'd worked in banking too long not to know it's serious, when someone tells you that you're going to need some form of identification. Even so, nothing could possibly have prepared me for what was about to happen over the next few days, after we met early in the afternoon of that Saturday, 5 May.

When I walked in to Cheryl and Harry's kitchen, the breakfast bar was covered in papers, scans from Mr and Mrs Ulrich's staff files. I recognised Mrs Ulrich's handwriting straightaway. I'd seen it often enough, when I was growing up. Cheryl had highlighted parts of some of the pages in bright yellow fluoro. She seemed pretty intense. I had the feeling she didn't want to muck around. We had to get on with this.

We went through the papers together quite quickly, just to get the gist of what they contained. Cheryl was pretty anxious for me to get a grip on it all because there was a form I needed to fill out. It was laid out on the benchtop too. Our whole focus was skimming through the pages to check for any mention of the name Cheryl had seen. Could it be my Mum?

Rather than cutting straight to the chase, as we did that day, I will try to quickly summarise the file contents here.

We read that the Ulrichs had sailed from Fremantle on 4 June 1937, to take up positions as OIC and nurse at Derby Native Hospital. Their contract was for one year. Clause 4 in the letter telling the Ulrichs of their appointment was the subject of some argument, in later correspondence, from Una F. Ulrich, in particular. That clause read:

> The whole of your time including Sundays and holidays if necessary, being at the disposal of the Department, you will at all times carry out the instructions of the Commissioner of Native Affairs (CNA) as may be conveyed to you by him or on his behalf.

In a letter dated 27 June 1937, Una wrote to the Commissioner of Native Affairs:

> ....our first impression of this place was so unfavourable, that my own desire was to return at once to the boat and give up all connection with your Department....
>
> ....Mr Kitson assured us both definitely that there would be domestic help at all the native hospitals. I find that is not so and my position here is that of cook – general (as well as nurse) for which position I do not aspire; nor is it one for which I have spent years of study and training...
>
> ...There is nothing in the wording of Clause 4 to prevent your demanding that I work 24 hours a day for 365 days and I will not subscribe to such a foolishness.

That letter, which the writer herself described as a lengthy discourse, was five pages long and much of it was about trying to convince the department to allow her to get some domestic help.

> Accommodation too, has to be considered, here I could have two half-caste girls and they would have a good home, having comfortable quarters in the same building as myself without encroaching on our privacy.
>
> I suggest two girls, they work better in pairs and this is a big place to keep clean and in order and also they need company. I think it would be a great success, especially as there is no colour bar in Derby – they could be taken to whatever social affairs were on and might eventually marry and become useful citizens – that, however, is going rather far ahead – more likely the local housewives would try and attract them away offering them higher wages.

She went on to ask if two girls were available at Moolabulla (also Moola Bulla), or even Moore River.

This information was all shooting over our heads as we skimmed through it. The choice of words was very different to what I was used to hearing. It was like we were reading about a different world. And where was Mum's world in all of this? There was no mention of Carnarvon, unless she had gone from Carnarvon to Moore River and ended up in Derby through that connection.

One year later, Hubert Ulrich wrote a more positive letter to the CNA.

> It is 12 months today since we arrived in Derby to more or less a horror of horrors. Our first letters to you were not very nice ones but I am very pleased to say that all of that is past forgotten.

> He went on to describe the building programme that had been started, writing
>
> ...we made up our minds that we were going to turn this place into something worthwhile, in fact turn (it) from the dirtiest and most dilapidated hospital and quarters into the best or as near the best as it is possible to make it.

Although 'there is still much work to be done', he sounds optimistic, pleased with what has been achieved and keen to continue, finishing with,

> Taking things right through, our work here has been a pleasure and most interesting and we hope that from your point of view it has been successful.

On 8 August 1938, there is a letter to the Aborigines Department, Government of Western Australia, praising the work being done at the Native Hospital and Mrs Ulrich, in particular. The letter is signed Albert P. Davis. Dr A.P. Davis was Medical Inspector of Aborigines at that time.

> I have been very pleased with the general air of contentment amongst the inmates of the Hospital and I think it only fair to state that this is due to the care and kindness of Mrs Ulrich who is tireless in her efforts to cure her patients.
>
> I think it only fair to tell you that she is doing all the treatment and doing it well. By that I mean she is carrying out that part of the treatment which is usually done by the Medical Officer and I am quite content that she should continue to do it. She is efficient and brings more enthusiasm to the work.
>
> Mr Ulrich also looks after his part of the Hospital efficiently. He has the interest of the natives at heart and I think, if you do not

> mind my making the suggestion, it might be more profitable to rely on him as a Protector than on the others in this town.

It is in another five-page letter, dated 18 August 1938, from Una F. Ulrich to the CNA, Mr. A.O. Neville, that we first find mention of Marjory.

> The Faulkners brought Agnes here on the 8th of this month. They had gone to Wyndham, whilst away.
>
> Agnes seems to have settled down very happily, in fact she seems to have made things happier for Kate and Marjory, who were not getting on very well and had had quite a fight a short time ago. However, they may be more peaceful with a third than with just the two girls.
>
> I am giving them (Marjory and Agnes) lessons daily, but will be glad when the correspondence lessons come for Marjory. Agnes would not take long to catch up to Marjory and they could easily do the same lessons – unless it is best to have separate studies for each from the correspondence Department. I don't suppose it would be any more expensive than sending them to school. If Agnes is to be enrolled it would mean finding a surname for her and filling in another form.
>
> Can Kate use Kitchener as a surname. It would be better if she could have a surname. It may seem a small thing, but Marjory has one and Kate who is older hasn't and it makes a little jealousy between them.

That 'Marjory has one …' grabbed my attention. The start of the next line caught my eye, too … 'Talking of half-castes … ' What was that supposed to mean? If this Marjory was Mum, did that term refer to her being half Chinese? Or was this something to do with that 13 per cent Melanesian in my DNA? Or both?

It looked as though the Melanesian DNA had come through Mum and if she was around 25 per cent, then one of her parents would have been around 50 per cent. I hadn't given much thought to this, but had to consider the possibility that maybe Mum's unknown mother had been part Aboriginal.

Once or twice, when we'd talked about Mum and I'd said I couldn't believe there was no record of her anywhere, basically right up until her marriage, there'd been the comment, 'It's like she was part of the Stolen Generation'. Cheryl and I had agreed but neither of us really believed that she had been. Mum looked so Chinese. And I still wasn't sure that this Marjory we were reading about was actually my mum. Was this all going to turn out to be yet another wild goose chase? Was I confused? Hmmmn … you could say that.

That letter ends with Mrs Ulrich writing that she intends to retain a supply of good-quality towelling to make towels for the girls and handtowels for use by staff and doctors, adding, 'The unbleached calico is a finer and better quality than usually supplied. I can use it to make under-clothes for Marjory and Agnes and night attire for them'. The mention of calico triggered a memory about Mum having used calico a lot in her sewing.

In April 1939, Mrs Ulrich writes that she is run-down, overworked and discouraged and questions whether she will stay on with the department, 'it is not worth it'. She is, however, convinced to stay on, only to resign again in a telegram sent on 1 July 1940.

(A.O. Neville had written to the Ulrichs in March, stating his intention to enter upon Long Service Leave prior to his retirement from the Public Service, thanking them for their service and loyalty to him and the department.)

Hubert Ulrich writes to the Acting Commissioner of Native Affairs, the same day, advising that the telegram was sent without his knowledge.

> I have now talked the matter over with her and convinced her that the present is not a suitable time to thrust changes on the Department and that I am not prepared to resign myself, at this or any other stage.

He adds that Mrs Ulrich is run-down and has been unwell for some weeks, '… but I feel that if extra help is forthcoming, very shortly things will probably adjust themselves satisfactorily'.

Two weeks later, Una withdraws her notice in a letter to the CNA, dated 16 July 1940, concluding, 'I have promised to carry on and I always keep my word'. The following day, she writes to Neville's successor Francis Bray, apologising for her hasty judgement, explaining that it was based on incorrect information, 'Thank you for your helpfulness and patience, I fear I am too impatient at times'. Marjory is mentioned again in this letter, another five pager.

> … when a bad case or a confinement comes, I may be (at the hospital) all day and half the night, just rushing down for meals and back again. The house must go on just the same when I am away – meals need preparing etc and so a dependable girl is needed to carry on without supervision during my absence. Marjory, although a mere school girl, has had to do this and has done very well indeed. However, I don't want to overwork her and also in the event of having any infant sent here from the Leprosarium, I felt an older girl would be necessary.

The letter also contains the comment: ' … if I did leave, I'd miss the children more than anything. I bring them up just as I would my own (if I had any) and we are really a little family in many ways.'

On 29 August 1940, Hubert Ulrich had also praised Marjory in a letter to the Acting CNA, 'Marjory, even with the little training she has had, is really an excellent girl, but is too young to be left on her own for any length of time.'

On 25 May 1941, Mrs Ulrich writes again to the CNA, stating '…it is essential that I have a few days off duty soon or I shall be a "cot case"'. She also appears very anxious about leaving the girls, 'little Gwen and Marjory'. 'Gwen is very attached to me and like Marjory does not want me to leave her here if I do not return.'

Then, on 9 September 1941, CNA Bray writes to the new OIC, Native Hospital, Derby, William Trigg,

> I have had a letter from Dr Musso. He tells me that you have had several letters from Mrs Ulrich. You may rest assured that Mrs Ulrich is not returning to Derby. Her services have been dispensed with.
>
> So far as I am concerned your services have been satisfactory, and I propose to retain you at Derby.

(Dr L.A. Musso, was Medical Inspector of Natives, Wyndham, according to a copy of a letter from Bray to Musso, 9 September 1941.)

On 14 October 1941, Bray forwards one of the letters to the Hon. Minister for the North-West, with the comment,

> … I am not aware of having spoken unfavourably about Mrs Ulrich. As a matter of fact I hold a high opinion of her as a Nurse but feel she was unsuited to the conditions at Derby. I propose to ignore the letter.

Similar advice is given to the Triggs after they write to Bray, on 2 December, requesting that he write to Mrs Ulrich and either request or order her to cease writing to Marjory King and Agnes Molloy.

That afternoon was the first time I'd seen the name Marjory King and I still was not sure if it was Mum. But I had to read on. What was the problem with Mrs Ulrich continuing to write to this girl, who could possibly have been Mum?

> It has taken quite a long while for the girls to get used to our ways but they are now very happy and contented here. But Mrs Ulrich by her letters is continually stirring up strife and making the girls discontented. The girls, Marjory in particular, are always unhappy and discontented after receiving a letter from Mrs Ulrich and it takes quite a while for them to get over it. Marjory has told us that she does not want to write to Mrs Ulrich and would prefer not to receive any letters from her. If you could force Mrs Ulrich to cease writing the girls would be far happier and contented. I am enclosing herewith the last letter Marjory received so you can see the class of letter being sent. Marjory gave it to me of her own freewill to send on to you.
>
> Yours faithfully,
>
> W.G. Trigg
>
> P.S. If any more letters come from Mrs Ulrich will you please advise me what to do with them. Shall I give them to Marjory or forward them to you unopened, or readdress them back to Mrs Ulrich unopened.
>
> Should you so request Dr Haynes is prepared to confirm this letter for it is upon his advice that I am appealing to you.

W.G. Trigg

The reply from Bray included the following:

> I think the better course to pursue would be to intercept and suppress all correspondence to your inmates by virtue of your

> power under Regulation 39. If you take charge of all letters coming from Mrs Ulrich and watch also to see that no letters are written to her by your inmates, I think the matter would gradually subside. I would recommend this course in preference to a letter from me to Mrs Ulrich. As previously stated, I would write to her if you would like me to, but consider it would be unwise to do so, as no doubt it would open up a flood of correspondence from her.

Inmates? I didn't like that word. When I first read it, I felt as if Mum must have been in some kind of jail. As if she was being punished for doing something wrong.

This was a lot to take in. Mrs Ulrich's letters had been intercepted. If Mum was this Marjory King, then how had Mrs Ulrich made contact later, to keep all those letters coming to our old place at West Swan. My head was spinning. Then I read the letter from Mrs Ulrich that W.G. Trigg had attached to his letter to Bray, which was dated 19 November 1941.

> My dear Marjory,
>
> I don't understand why you have not had my letters …
>
> Don't they give you any ink to write with. You must either get ink or write with a darker pencil for I can hardly read your little letter to me. It was sweet of you to remember Boss's birthday. I will send him the handkerchief and he will be pleased to get it.
>
> I wish you could find time to write me a letter with news in it. You don't tell me anything, why is that dear, won't they let you?
>
> Mrs Maywood has been worried for a long time over no lessons coming from Gwen and Agnes and she wrote to them and has had no reply. I hope Agnes finished her fourth class lessons.

The whole thing is terribly wrong I know. But that must happen when people don't know much and think they know everything.

Oh, never mind, as long as you remember my words and keep yourself decent and try to do what is right, it is all that you can do for the present. The war must be dealt with first. I am trying to help you all but the war makes it harder.

I do wish you were with me. I often think of you and of Agnes and Gwen and long to be with you. Is Dinah still there and what about Chugera. Did you hear of Friday, Gilgie, Polly or anyone else I know. How are the goats and the birds (poor little sweeties). Is pink-top alright and what about my little Smoky. I hope he is still well. Have you heard from your Mother, did she get my letter. Did Gwen get a birthday card from me – I posted her one.

Did you get all the parcels – how do you like the letters for sewing on your things – I put one for Gwen on a washer to show you how. You could see the two letters were for your names – M.K. and A.M.

I do hope you get this letter and I expect a long letter in reply. If they won't give you any ink you will have to buy a bottle. How is Bessie and where is she? Did you give Dinah the parcel of dresses I sent her – did she like them? Marjory Darling – don't lose heart. I need a longer rest, I am not very well and it is perhaps a good thing I can stay away from the North a little longer.

I have had a bad cough and cold but it is better now since I got home again.

Cheer up dear ones – Sister still loves you and misses you.

Love to you all from your loving Sister.

This was all a bit too much to take in at once. Quite a few things didn't add up. The letter had been written on 19 November, six days before Mum's birthday, which was supposedly 25 November. But there was no mention of Mum's birthday in the letter, even though two other birthdays had been mentioned, Gwen's and Boss's. Presumably Boss was Mr Ulrich. And what about that line, 'Have you heard from your Mother, did she get my letter.'

What was all that about? If this Marjory was Mum then this was the first I'd heard about her mother. Or rather, the second time, if you count that page in Cheryl's mother's diary, where Marj had mentioned that her mother died when she was 10. But Mum had turned 10 in 1934, which matched when Kimbly Quan Sing had died, yet this letter from Mrs Ulrich was written in 1941. Could this 'Mother' even refer to Una Quan Sing?

The only thing I was certain of was that Mrs Ulrich believed this Marjory King's mother was still alive in 1941. And it looks like her mother could read. Why else would Mrs Ulrich write to her?

Then Cheryl showed me a list of names. The name Marjorie King was on it and there was a number against it. This was the file number! All I had to do was fill out the Family History Application Form and send it in. My mind went into overdrive, filling out that form. Then, we drafted a letter to the director of the Aboriginal History Research Unit.

I had to assume that the Marjory King associated with Mrs Ulrich was the Marjorie King on file and that this same person was Mum. It was a lot to take in. We had been led up the garden path and got nowhere, so many times. And although the DNA had hinted at some

Melanesian heritage, I hadn't really factored it into this mix. The DNA hadn't told us a great deal. I'd only had a couple of matches with any Melanesian connections. And one of them had turned out to be another red herring. But I had to assume this Marjory was Mum in order to apply.

In the letter to accompany the application, I explained the circumstances, as we knew them, up until that point.

> For many years I have been trying to find out more about Mum's early history and discover the identity of my maternal grandparents. It is as though Mum did not exist until 1948 when she married my father. No birth record for her has ever been found although she believed she was born in Derby in November, 1924. Whenever asked about her childhood Mum became upset to the point where I felt reluctant to ask further questions.
>
> I do have in my possession a cook book that was given to Mum in 1940 by Sister Una F. Ulrich. Mrs Ulrich maintained a friendship with Mum for many years; she was present at the birth of one of my brothers and in old age travelled by bus from Queensland to stay with us and attend my sister's wedding in 1975.
>
> Last week, through a friend researching at the State Records Office, I learned that Mrs Ulrich was Matron and her husband Hubert OIC at Derby Native Hospital for about two years, from June 1937.
>
> Marjory King is mentioned as a schoolgirl working as a domestic servant for the Ulrichs during that time. The name Marjorie King is also contained on the Names Index … the corresponding number is also close to those of other girls mentioned on the

files as working for the Ulrichs at the same time. This would have been around the time Mum was given the cook book by Mrs Ulrich.

I have no idea who my mother's parents were and would very much like to know. My Dad was descended from Western European/Irish stock and that family line is well known to me. Mum was part-Chinese and the surname Quan Sing was mentioned in rumours as possibly being connected to our family. Recently, I completed a DNA test which has come back suggesting that one of Mum's parents was indeed possibly a Quan Sing; my ethnicity estimate included 21% Asia East and I have close matches with several of the current generation of Quan Sings. Rumours include that Kinverns (Lanky) Quan Sing may have been Mum's father, however another option is that one of his sisters was Mum's mother. The Quan Sings were storekeepers in Derby and Carnarvon at the time Mum was born.

It would appear that her other parent was half European and half-Aboriginal. This is based on my DNA results (13% Melanesian) and also the comment in one of Mrs Ulrich's letters where she writes 'Talking of half-castes … ' immediately after writing about Marjory and the other girls employed as domestics.

It was always believed that 'King' was a name given to Mum by Mrs Ulrich. Her birth date may also be a guesstimate. In the Ulrich staff files at the SRO Mrs Ulrich wrote in 1938 to A.O. Neville suggesting surnames for one of the other girls employed with Marjory at that time.

I also have a copy of my parents' marriage certificate where Mum's parents are listed as Father: Unknown, Mother: Annie Dantau King? (difficult to read).

> Mum did tell me that she attended Lawley Ladies' College, a hostel for country girls, in Mt Lawley. This was run by two sisters, Miss Rosalie Ross Sharp and Miss Mabel Ross Sharp. I remember the two Miss Sharps driving out to visit Mum when we lived at West Swan in the early 1960s.
>
> After leaving school Mum worked as a nursing aide at the Mount Hospital in Perth, until her marriage. I hope you are able to help fill in the many gaps in Mum's family story …

Once we were happy with the contents of the letter, we printed out some supporting information including a photograph of Mrs Ulrich with Mum, taken by a street photographer in Perth. Then we scanned the inside cover of Mum's old *Golden Wattle Cookery Book* to show the inscription in Mrs Ulrich's handwriting. It was then that we took a closer look at the smudge right under Mrs Ulrich's signature. Someone had rubbed out whatever it was that had been written there. It looked as though the ink had been rubbed away with an eraser or maybe even breadcrumbs. Looking more closely at it, the faint outline of the word could just be made out. Derby.

10

WAITING

– CR –

Text messages and emails kept the threads of communication alive, because the lives we led back then made this virtually impossible otherwise. Jennifer was working full time in Perth and I was caught up with the demands of horticulture and three generations of family, back in the Swan Valley and always trying to write in amongst it all. But about twice a year, we tried to meet for dinner at The Rose and Crown in Guildford, in person, just the two of us for a proper catch-up.

Tuesday, 8 May 2018 seemed an opportune time for one of those talkfests. So much had happened in the previous few days that we had a lot to sort through. Besides, it was a celebration of sorts. Jennifer had submitted her application for the Marjorie King file and maybe that would lead somewhere new. I even took along the Ulrich files to dinner, but we didn't end up studying the contents, that night.

It was a chance to fill Jennifer in, on an exciting couple of days at the State Records Office. There hadn't been much time to talk about that, the previous Saturday, as there'd been too much reading and thinking to do. The Battye Library had given me the email address for the Aboriginal History Research Unit, but the catch was the unit was in the process of setting-up a new office on the second floor of the State Library and was not yet open to the public. The delay had felt like yet another setback, but an email to Dr Chris Owen had brought a reply within half an hour with application forms attached.

> …in regards Jennifer's query probably the best place to start is for her to fill out the attached Family History Application and we will undertake a comprehensive investigation into her family history that will include a detailed genealogy. We know there is quite an extensive King family in the North West/Kimberley and what were known as Personal History Cards that were part of the Aboriginal Welfare system of the time exists for Marjory King.
>
> Due to privacy provisions, Jennifer will have to fill this out herself and provide some information.

We talked about this, as we drank and ate during an enjoyable couple of hours. As usual, the food was delicious, even if the sudden delivery of information overload was proving to be a lot harder to digest. Debriefing would take time. There was too much to take in. All at once. Neither of us could possibly have imagined what was about to happen next.

The gods had woken up.

11

10 MAY

– JD –

On Wednesday, 9 May 2018, Cheryl had sent me a text message, the morning after our dinner, at the Rose and Crown.

> *Enjoyed our dinner thanks. And Mr Wm George Trigg was shorter than Mr Ulrich....5'5". After Derby he spent time at the Anglican Children's Home in Middle Swan and died aged 71 in 1971 at Parkerville....maybe Parkerville Children's Home? His wife Ellen was also a nurse.*

The Anglican Children's Home in Middle Swan was familiar to me. It later became Swanleigh Hostel, for country high school kids. At Hampton Senior High School, in the Seventies, there had been many Swanleighans among my classmates.

By this stage, I had learned that the Marjorie King whose file I'd applied for had worked for Mr and Mrs Trigg in Derby. Then he'd spent time at the place I knew as Swanleigh. I wondered whether Mum had known this, assuming she was the same Marjorie King. Swanleigh was only a few minutes away from our place in West Swan.

We were still trying to identify the man in the wedding photograph, the man who had apparently escorted Mum to the altar. Mr Trigg, at 5 ft 5 ins, didn't seem to have the height. At least we could cross him off the list.

But I had more pressing matters on my mind. Like the file I'd just applied to get. 'Thx what were the words the Dr said about Mum's file?' Although I used the word Mum's, I still wasn't sure it *was* my Mum.

> We know there is quite an extensive King family in the North West/Kimberley and what were known as Personal History Cards that were part of the Aboriginal Welfare system of the time exists for Marjory King.

All of this renewed activity must have stirred Cheryl to check in on my DNA results, because that Wednesday night she messaged through an update.

> Just checked the DNA and you have your first shared match with Munya. Someone called AJ. Worth remembering when the questions start down the track.

She meant the questions that would inevitably start, once I got hold of that Marjorie King file. I could hardly wait.

Munya Andrews' DNA test had come up as a distant match with mine and we knew she had been born in Derby like Mum. For a long time, there had been no other shared matches with the tiny cluster that was Munya and me.

I wanted to be ahead of the game, so early next morning I messaged Cheryl again,

> Hey, can I have Munya's last name and the % or whatever of the DNA or what relationship we are, 1st or 2nd cuz.

The reply came back early the next day, Thursday, 10 May,

> Munya Andrews. Possible range 4th to 6th cousin. Confidence high ... AJ is ... confidence good, also possible range 4th to 6th cousins. Her ethnicity is Melanesia, Great Britain, Asia South, Asia East. Did you want me to msg AJ and ask if she knows of any family connections with NWest WA?

'Why not, can not hurt asking,'

When another text message from Cheryl quickly followed, it put the wind up me a bit.

'Hi Jennifer. When are you able to talk? Cx'

Cheryl never contacted me during working hours. She had this thing about not wanting to put me off my work. I dealt with big numbers and she didn't want me getting a decimal point in the wrong place. My gut reaction was that someone had died.

I was sitting at our team's work station, part of a team of six at Bankwest in Perth, with two tables each of three colleagues, facing each other. Our team leader Mitch, was seated in the middle, on the opposite table.

We each had double screens set up, and I had my mobile phone set on silent, propped up on the desk beside me. That way, I could deal with a text message, without disturbing any of the others in the team. I responded, 'Can call you now if you like.'

To make the call, meant going to what we called The Quiet Room. It was a soundproof room just behind the work station and was where anyone went when they had to deal with personal stuff, like the family cat being run over. Whenever anyone went there, the others in the team knew something was up.

I called Cheryl and straightaway, she asked if I'd checked my emails. 'There's one from Julie,' she said. 'You really need to see this, now.' Cheryl's tone was quite firm. I sensed that she thought this was important, but had no idea what it was about.

Less than a minute later, back at my desk, I read what Julie's forwarded email said and it all very slowly started to sink in. My mind was just skipping across the surface of everything I was reading. It would be ages before the significance of times and dates and players would truly register. There was just too much to comprehend at once.

I read Julie's message attached to a forwarded message, first.

Hello Cheryl and Jennifer,

Thank you Cheryl for your last email and sorry I haven't replied earlier. I have been re-reading it all and taking it all in. I would be keen to see what turns out once Jennifer you get access to the records.

This obviously related to our update to Julie on my application to get hold of the Marjorie King file. Understandably, Julie would be interested, but I didn't really see why her request warranted me stopping work.

Now, coincidentally Jeremy has just sent me the attached email which sort of lines up with your investigations. Shall I direct the chap who contacted Jeremy to you? Or what or who do you suggest would be useful?

Cheers

PS Welcome back Jennifer and Geoff. Hope the holiday was enjoyable.

Julie

The forwarded message from Julie's nephew, Jeremy, followed. He'd received it the previous afternoon, and later on the same night he had forwarded it to his Dad, Gary, who had been involved in the flaming drum incident, and his Auntie Julie.

> Hi Dad and Auntie Julie
>
> I received the email below from someone who is doing some research into the stolen generation. Apparently he is trying to track down someone (i.e an indigenous person removed from their family) who lived with the Quan Sings in Derby and Carnarvon in the 1930s-1940s!
>
> Who do you think I should put this person in contact with to see if anyone remembers anything? Either of you?
>
> Cheers

As the page scrolled down, I then read the email that had triggered all of this. It was from James Feehan, a caseworker with the Kimberley Stolen Generation Aboriginal Corporation (KSGAC), based in Broome. James had emailed Jeremy, late on Wednesday. He had targeted Jeremy after doing a search of the name Quan Sing.

Here's what James wrote:

> Hi Jeremy,
>
> I did speak with your office earlier however they informed me that you are quite busy.
>
> I am a Link Up Caseworker for Kimberley Stolen Generation in Broome WA. I am currently working on a case that has links to the Quan Sing Family (from Derby and then on to Carnarvon, WA) and was hoping to chat to you further on the matter.
>
> I am researching on behalf of a client, in an effort to locate a lost family member who lived with the Quan Sings in Derby originally before they relocated to Carnarvon with them – possibly in the 1930s–40s.

I was hoping I could make contact with someone from this family who may have some knowledge or possible leads I could follow up.

If you are able to assist I would welcome a reply at your earliest.

Kind Regards,

James Feehan.

As soon as I read this, it slowly started to sink in. 'Oh My God … I think I've found my mother's family.'

It is hard to describe how excited I felt in that brief moment. If the person James was searching for was Mum, then it meant she had Aboriginal family out there and they'd been searching too. I felt both ecstatic and in shock. And did I mention confused? According to what James had written, this lost family member had lived with the Quan Sings in Derby and had moved to Carnarvon with them. This seemed to fit what Mum had told me, but it still didn't explain why we'd never been able to find anyone in Carnarvon who remembered Mum. Especially not the Quan Sings. And then, I started to cry.

I guess it was all too much to take in all at once, after so many years of nothing. And as excited as I was about a possible Aboriginal connection, my next feeling was one of dread. 'I am going to cop all the racial shit.'

All the other members of the team were well aware, by now, that something big had happened. They'd twigged that something was up. Then, there was this meltdown at my desk.

Mitch was up and out of his seat, in full Team Leader mode, wanting to know what was up, and what he could do to help. The support that I had from all my work colleagues, through all that was to come, was absolutely amazing.

I called Cheryl straightaway.

'Do you think I should call this James?'

'Definitely.'

My mouth was dry and my hands were shaking. James didn't know me, so I had to introduce myself.

'Hi James,

'My name is Jennifer Durrant. I have just received an email from Julie QuanSing-Rowlands, forwarding an email her nephew received from your office. I think you may have been looking for my Mum, Marjorie.'

The response from James floored me.

'I have two clients who have been looking for your Mum for years. They promised their mother they would never give up the search for Marjorie.'

James asked quite a few more questions. He really needed to verify that Mum was the right person. I told him that on the previous Saturday I'd applied to the West Australian Government for the Marjorie King file, but hadn't yet received it. James said he was aware of Dr Chris Owen and his department, but his inquiry was independent of my application. He had no knowledge of it. Nor had he known of Mum's surname King.

So much was happening. There were quite a few telephone conversations that morning. James needed more identifying documentation. He had to be absolutely sure he had the right person. If he could verify it all, then he would work towards a reunion. Then, all I had to do was confirm the connection between Mum and me.

At some point, he asked where Mum was. He meant, where Mum was buried, because once everything was verified he would work towards sending his clients down to Perth for a graveside farewell.

'You can't do that,' I told him.

He sounded a bit surprised. 'Why not?'

'Because she's sitting on a shelf, in the front room…'

There was silence on the other end of the line. I felt some explanation was necessary.

'We had Mum cremated eleven years ago, but then we couldn't make a final decision about what to do with the ashes. So she's been sitting in the front room ever since.'

James's response took a while to sink in.

'In that case, you might need to come up to Broome, to return your Mum to country.'

By lunchtime, my whole world seemed to have turned on its head. This was the follow-up to the first conversation, which I'd had with the caseworker, James.

> It was great to connect with you today. As I mentioned, I am working with a client who has been looking for Marjorie for a long time.
>
> Our research contacts led me to the Quan Sings as it is understood Annie D'Antoine (B. 1891, Derby, WA) had a child with a Quan Sing, and the child is believed to be Marjorie. It is understood that Marjorie travelled with Quan Sing's brother's family (Ayling??) to Carnarvon. After that I have no idea where she went.
>
> My client (who would be a half-niece to Marjorie) took on her mother's (who would be half-sister to Marjorie) case as she was also looking before passing away.
>
> I would love the opportunity to work with you in more detail on this to fully confirm any connections. As a caseworker, I abide by strict adherence to confidentiality of, and respect for, any

information exchanged and act as the mediator for any possible reunion.

At some point, another call from James came. When he told me what he'd found out, I literally could not speak. This was the moment, when I knew with absolute certainty that we were both talking about Mum.

'Your mother had a scar on her left knee, where she was bitten by a shark.'

James had found the little girl who was with Mum the day she was bitten. I would soon hear that story firsthand. But in that particular moment, I was dumbfounded. It was like I'd been struck by lightning all over again and this time, it had hit home. I'd never shared any information with James about those big, silver scars around Mum's left knee. The scars that I'd been told were the result of a shark attack, when she was about 15 and living in Carnarvon. Carnarvon was figuring in all of these conversations, but not everything was clear-cut.

Mention of the Aylings was a bit of a puzzle. Cheryl had checked the Quan Sing information and found that Lanky's sister, Sideral Quan Sing, had married William Ayling, but this was not until November, 1943. Mum would have been about to turn 19, by this stage. And the Aylings had married in Perth, it seemed they hadn't moved to Derby, until later. Glenis had found a 1944 letter giving her parents' address as Hay Street, Perth. It was not until 1946 that advertisements had started appearing for Ayling Quan Sing, general store and refreshment rooms, in Derby.

Mitch had been tuned in to all of this and at some stage, he must have been checking out the policy with Human Resources. The bank has a number of initiatives supporting reconciliation with Aboriginal and Torres Strait Islander people. I was aware of this because I'd been on the training courses. It had just never crossed my mind that it might apply to me.

Mitch came with me that day to see my manager, once it had been suggested that I might need to take Mum's ashes up north. He'd already printed out the policy. I told my manager that I'd just discovered that my Mum was part of the Stolen Generation. I needed five days' leave and I only had two days of leave left after the recent holiday in Hong Kong and Singapore. And we were just approaching the end of the financial year. What we call financial month is a busy, busy time. Staff are usually not allowed to take leave during this busy time. But after hearing the story, my manager said five days was no problem, 'How can we possibly say no?'

By mid-afternoon, Cheryl and I were trying to work out what supporting evidence I could send James, and there had been a message from her.

> ... The marriage certificate naming Annie Dantau ???? King as mother might be enough. I think I have a scan of it at home and can email it to you later. And your DNA puts your closest rellie as Julie, first to second cousin equivalent which fits with Lanky being Nugget's brother. The scan of the cookbook inscription puts your mother in Derby in 1940. The extract of one of Mrs U's letters gives Marj's surname as King. I'd send him the lot, including pic of Mrs U and Marj as a young woman. His client may see a likeness ...

And the day still wasn't done. After work, there was another message from Cheryl,

'There's more....AJ your new match has answered this morning's msg. She lives at One Arm Point, which is 220 km from Broome.'

I looked up One Arm Point and it was way, way north of Broome. I thought, no way was that match going to be of any significance.

The days stretched into weeks, around all of this happening, and time became a blur. My caseworker James was away the following week, working at Halls Creek. By then, I'd sent him all the supporting evidence I had, so I turned my attention back to Mum's file.

When I hadn't heard anything back by Mother's Day, I decided to give Dr Chris Owen a call. He told me that my application had been received and was being processed. The whole department was dealing with a huge backlog of work and Mum's quite substantial file was part of that.

When another week went by with nothing, I was champing at the bit. I emailed Dr Owen on 22 May, asking how my inquiry was going. It also gave me a chance to update him.

> Since sending in my application there has been a development and a case worker from the Kimberley Stolen Generation Aboriginal Corporation is also working on behalf of clients that may be related to my Mother.
>
> Can you please advise when any information on my Mother will be available.
>
> Please advise what the process is?
>
> Thank you.

Reading it again now, I'm glad it makes sense. At the time, I could barely think or type straight. I sent that off and had a response an hour later. Dr Owen apologised for the delay. Moving offices had created a bit of a backlog of work to catch up with.

> That said, I'm looking at your application now. You are in luck as your mother has an entire 200 page 'Personal File' from the

> Department of Native Welfare from 1937. (We only received these files late last year.) The card you refer to in your letter.... is the corresponding Personal History Card for Marjory which explains that her mother was HC (Half-caste) 'Annie' from Sunday Island Mission and her father was a Chinese man from Derby named Quan Sing.
>
> It appears Marjory was given the (name) King by the well-known A.O. Neville, after King Sound, which is where she came from...Apparently she couldn't take the name Sing because of the Chinese connotations. It appears she was taken from Sunday Island Mission to be trained and sent to school by Mrs Ulrich of the Derby Hospital.
>
> I'll review the file and you should have it soon. Just a word of warning, the file contains the racism common to the period.

I couldn't get on to my computer quick enough. And there was Sunday Island, inside King Sound, right opposite One Arm Point (now Ardyaloon). Where AJ, my new DNA match with Munya Andrews, lived. Who knew?

Later, there was another email from Dr Chris, as I now thought of him.

> Well, I've dug a bit deeper. Annie was Annie Ah Chu, who was married to Bob Ah Chu. Annie's parents were...'Frenchy' D'Antoine ... and a 'fullblood' woman known as Nundra. We just need to process this and we will post it out or you can come and pick it up, we are in the State library.

Oh My God! I had been waiting almost forty years for this. Dr Chris said he would drop me a message when the file was ready. It might take a few days.

Dr Chris had sent through my family tree information headed Ancestors of Jennifer York. The information tracked back from me as Generation 1 down through Generation 2, which was the known information about Mum and Dad and my brothers and sister. It was amazing to see so much information about Generations 3, 4 and 5, written down in front of me. Some of it I'd only recently learned about and much of it was new.

For the first time, I could read about Mum's mother and my grandmother Annie D'Antoine and her parents. My maternal great-grandparents. The information stated that Annie was born in 1896, on Sunday Island Mission and had died there on 19 February 1960. Annie's father was Adrian 'Frenchy' D'Antoine, and her mother Nundra, born about 1882, had died in 1957, the year I was born.

I forwarded the family tree information on to Cheryl and she picked up another coincidence. Today was 22 May, the 87th anniversary of 'Frenchy' D'Antoine's death in Broome.

James called me the following day to suggest that I make telephone contact with the two ladies who'd been looking for Mum all that time. They were the daughters of Mum's half-sister Maggie Davey and their names were Dorothy Hunter (born 1955) and Margaret Davey (born 1947). (Margaret has since passed away.)

What floored me most of all was how, all of a sudden, these two lines of inquiry had come together. James also wanted to know how I felt about all of this. I told him I was overwhelmed, and uncertain about the cultural side of it all. How was I supposed to address people? What was culturally correct? And politically incorrect? He said I would be considered a sister. There are no halves!

He was looking at having the reunion, the following month, some time in June. At that stage, it was still not certain whether it would be in Perth or in Broome. I really needed to find out soon because I had to let work know. It was sorted that day, as far as the reunion was concerned. James would organise everything. I didn't have to worry about a thing. I would soon be taking Mum's ashes to Broome.

I'd decided to wait until the following Sunday to call Margaret and Dorothy. I needed time to get myself together. This had been a long time coming. Early Sunday morning, Cheryl sent me a text message to wish me luck.

> Good luck this afternoon. As a good omen today you have a new 4th to 6th cousin match in the Seychelles and they have a D'Antoine in their tree born c. 1830.

We knew, by this time, that the D'Antoine line was strongly represented in the Seychelles. Some of the ducks were starting to line up.

James just had to check it all out with all concerned. He was hoping to take me to One Arm Point and to Derby. I'd decided to scan some photographs of Mum and put them in an album for the family to keep.

As well as that project on the go, I was getting anxious again about getting Mum's file. I really wanted to see it before I went up to the Kimberley. Not that there was a lot of spare time to read it. I was required to produce a current medical certificate in order to travel to Broome. This was when I discovered that my blood pressure had spiked a bit. This was unusual. It concerned me, but I soon learned that it was a symptom of the pressure I was under. By early June, my Broome dates were confirmed. I'd be leaving on 17 June to take Mum home.

Then I had a message from Dr Chris, Mum's file was ready for collection. I arranged to collect it in person, on Thursday, 7 June.

Cheryl was coming along for moral support. All I could think about was picking up that file. At work, that morning, I kept glancing at my watch trying so hard to focus, but all I could think about was that soon I would be picking up the file that would explain Mum's early years. My mouth was dry and my heart was racing. I had never done anything like this before and had no idea what to expect.

All I was hoping was that Mum had not been abused in any way. I'd heard so many stories about people being mistreated and beaten during that time, whether they were escaping the war or among those that were taken. I just hoped that Mum had been okay. The abuse issue was weighing very heavily on my mind.

It was raining when I headed across the forecourt towards the State Library. Cheryl had seen me heading across the pavers towards the glass entry doors, head down, brolly up, but then I'd disappeared. She went out to see where I'd gone and I was standing outside the entrance, practising deep breathing.

Once I got my act together, we went inside and up to the reception desk to ask for Dr Owen. Within minutes, he'd arrived in the foyer carrying Mum's file. It was then that he mentioned that around 17,000 files had been released only recently in late 2017.

Knowing that the files had only become available relatively recently would later be a huge relief to me and Cheryl says she feels the same. In all those early years I'd been looking, we would never have found it even if we'd known what we were looking for.

Even though my heart was going like a jackhammer and I could barely think, I was aware of the respect that was shown in the way the file was presented. Obviously, a lot of work had gone into putting the information together for me. The folder was labelled My Family History, with my name typed underneath. The folder was offered to me, then I took it. The formal handover of my family history was complete. With the trip to the Kimberley, now just days away, I was way too busy to do much more than skim through the contents of Mum's file, let alone digest it.

I had a couple of goes at reading it and trying to make sense of it all, but I had a bad case of information overload. What I do remember from that initial attempt to understand the contents is the awareness that it really only covered Mum's life from when she was about 14 years old to around 21 years. I still didn't know anything really about Mum's first 14 years. What sort of childhood did she have?

Maybe I'd learn more when I took Mum back to the Kimberley. I was expecting there would be some sort of a quiet, scattering of ashes ceremony and had to prepare myself for that. And new family to meet. There was the photograph album to compile, a speech to write, for whatever was being planned for Mum and I was still working five days a week. It was around this time that I took our house off the market – it was another stress I just didn't need. The spike in my blood pressure had also been worrying me, so I booked a check at a pharmacy the weekend after picking up the file. But by then it was back to normal.

Then on 13 June, I messaged Cheryl with the news that I'd received the plane tickets and the room confirmation. But a couple of hours later, there was another message.

'Have you read the latest email from Julie?'

I couldn't believe what I was reading. It gave me the weirdest feeling of deja vu. A family history research officer with an Aboriginal Corporation based in Perth was chasing information about the Quan Sing history in Derby. That set in motion another flurry of activity. I wondered if Mum's nieces had been making inquiries through this organisation too. But when I called James, he knew nothing about it.

If she wasn't working for the two ladies I was about to meet, then maybe there were even more relatives out there than I realised. How much more could I handle?

In the end, it turned out to be another red herring. The email had been triggered by an inquiry from someone else trying to connect with their family. The names, places and time line I gave them were not a match.

But the event did give rise to a comment 'The old souls are moving', and that still seems true to me now.

It would be two and a half years before Cheryl, Julie and I would get together to discuss all that happened in May, 2018. I'd gone over to Cheryl and Harry's place the previous day, to go through the Ulrich files together, to try to recreate what we'd done on that Saturday afternoon that had ended with me posting my application to access the Marjorie King file. Then I was recounting to Cheryl all that had happened on 10 May – that day at work when everything seemed to be happening at once. So much had happened in the space of a few hours on that one particular day. It still feels to me, as though weeks were condensed into those hours. I kept repeating the date, 10 May. I was racking my brain for a connection. I guess the spiritual side of me was looking for a sign, and not coming up with anything.

Julie joined us the following day. I hadn't really had the chance to bring her up to speed on all that had happened, particularly on my reunions in the north. Usually we meet in a group – on her own it was easier for both of us to share information. There were so many questions from all sides. Another reason for the visit was to pick Julie's brains about the Quan Sing family, to flesh out the family members relevant to this story.

Then just after lunch when we were more relaxed, Julie pulled out her iPad. She and her husband Richard had recently been back to Carnarvon and had made a tour of the places of family significance. Julie showed us photographs of the old Quan Sing store site. The store has long gone, but there is a marker stone on the spot telling some of the story of the site's connection to the family.

They had also visited the property where her parents Nugget and Lily had the banana plantation and had shared some of its story with the current owners. The rustic old shed was still there and she told us how the family had packed beans inside its walls when she was a child. When very young, she had accepted her Dad's challenge to grow a bean crop, 'from go to woe', and had planted, tended and packed one row of beans, for the princely reward of £1.

Last, she showed us a photograph of Lanky Quan Sing's headstone. This was of interest, of course. Julie told us again what a kind man he was, always trying to help people.

Anyone, who knows me, will tell you that it's not often I'm lost for words. But for a few moments, after taking in what was written on Lanky's headstone, I was.

We all were.

Lanky's date of birth?

10 May.

12

MUNYA

– CR –

When Jennifer's DNA test results first came back, on 19 December 2015, the most exciting observation was that she had a match with a W.D. Schulze. When that match was confirmed as being with Wendy, daughter of Doris Schulze, we felt that, as far as the Quan Sing line was concerned, the search was on track.

Wendy's match came in with 63 per cent probability as a second cousin (or equivalent). Assuming Marj's father was Lanky who was a brother to Doris's mother Zephyr Quan Sing Scott, then Jennifer and Wendy are indeed second cousins. This small but heady success encouraged Jennifer to see whether Julie would be willing to do a DNA test in a bid to fine-tune her links with the Quan Sing line. Julie would end up doing the DNA test in early 2018.

Meanwhile, there were other avenues to explore in Jennifer's results. Her ethnicity approximations for a start, about 62 per cent European, and 22 per cent Asian, mainly Asia East. These seemed to fit what she knew about Henry York's ancestral line and also that Marjorie had probably been about half Chinese. What about that other, unknown half?

Initially, under the heading Pacific Islander, Jennifer's ethnicity came up as 13 per cent Melanesia. Later, when Julie's test results first came in, her ethnicity estimate was 89 per cent Asia East and 11 per cent Polynesia. The Polynesia/Melanesia reference in both Jennifer and Julie's test results, under the heading Pacific Islander, led us to think there must have been some DNA connection with this area through the Quan Sing line. Melanesia, Micronesia and Polynesia are represented by three groups of islands in the Pacific Ocean to the north and east of Australia.

What we could not foresee then was that DNA analysis is being refined and updated, all the time. A spokesperson for Ancestry recently told me that it is only since March 2019 that they have been able to distinguish Aboriginal and Torres Strait Islander DNA as distinct from Melanesian.

> DNA ethnicity estimates are updated from time to time based on advances in DNA science and an increasing number of samples in our reference panel. With each update, we continue to add new regions, making results even more precise. This update would explain why your friend has seen a change in their ethnicity results.

Julie's updated ethnicity result is now 100 per cent Asia East, which pleases her. 'I know I am 100 per cent Chinese,' she has always told us.

Jennifer's main ethnicity estimates now read 42 per cent England and North-West Europe, 23 per cent Southern China, 13 per cent Aboriginal and Torres Strait Islander, a smattering of Germanic

Europe, Ireland, Spain, Sweden and just one per cent Melanesian (range zero to three per cent).

The fine-tuning that specifically identified that Aboriginal and Torres Strait Islander DNA happened after March 2019, by which time Jennifer had already solved the puzzle of Marjorie's identity through other means.

Since 10 May 2018, there's been an awful lot going on with regard to Marj's story. Nonetheless, the term Melanesian had sparked some interest. As vague as it was then, it did give rise to the faint thought that we had to consider the possibility Marj may have had some indigenous Australian heritage. But who? What? When? And where?

We knew Lanky was full Chinese, but knew nothing of Marj's mother. One possibility was that Lanky had been in a relationship with a woman who was part Aboriginal. He would have been 22 when Marj was conceived and although, based in Carnarvon by then, it was reasonable to expect that he had continued to visit Derby where the Quan Sing family still had a connection.

At this earlier stage, we had not discounted Una Quan Sing as a possibility for Marj's mother either. There was well-documented evidence that she had pushed hard at the laws of the day in her bid to employ Aboriginal people. The possibility that she may have had a relationship with an Aboriginal man was still on our radar, back then.

Trawling through Jennifer's initial matches took time. It meant going through each match, checking ethnicity and trying to work out how each person fitted into Jennifer's DNA story. Matches with public family trees were useful, because they provided more clues about names in their ancestral line. It was helpful that Jennifer's York line had been so well researched, making names in that paternal line easy to identify.

What we were really looking for was someone, who was a match with Jennifer, had Melanesian DNA and had no shared matches with anyone related through her paternal line. It took some time to work through all the stats and reach the point where we found Munya Andrews who, back then, was 27th on Jennifer's list of matches.

Looking at a printed version of Jennifer's initial test results now, I see that I'd written NSM, no shared matches, next to Munya's name. Whatever DNA they shared was unique to their small cluster of two. Even so, it seemed a long shot. Their predicted relationship showed as fourth to sixth cousins or equivalent. That shared DNA seemed mighty small. The best hope was the 30 per cent probability that they were third cousins, second cousins twice removed, half second cousins once removed, or half first cousins three times removed.

It seemed like we were going to have to wade through a great number of ancestors to establish the link and in Marj's case, we had only her mother's name as shown on her marriage certificate, a name that looked like Annie Dantau.

We were hesitant about contacting Munya with such flimsy information. But when I clicked on her profile, she had written that she was willing to help other members with their research. That was encouraging. Then I typed Munya's name into a search engine. Wow! To quote her Wikipedia profile,

> Munya Andrews is a Bardi woman from the Kimberley region of Western Australia. She trained as a lawyer and has worked in academia and comedy. Among her interests she lists parachuting, bungee jumping and flying.

I liked that Munya mentioned comedy. And soon discovered that she is also a writer of note, having written *Journey Into Dreamtime*, described as an easy guide to Aboriginal spirituality that informs readers about Dreamtime concepts, in a simple way.

Now based in Sydney, Munya is co-director of business consultancy Evolves that specialises in Indigenous cultural awareness and training. Munya describes her life purpose as creating better understanding and appreciation of Aboriginal people and to leave behind a legacy of Dreamtime wisdom for future generations. On the Evolves website, this positive and co-operative philosophy is summed up by the statement:

> Together we are evolving a kinder world that celebrates our shared humanity, we transform conflict to connection, alienation to belonging and fear to celebration. WOOHOO!

The information I could find online certainly eased any trepidation I may have felt about making contact – Jennifer's match was extremely distant. The clincher was noticing that Munya was born in Derby. So I sent off a message on 11 February 2017.

> Hello Munya – I administer the DNA test for my old friend, Jennifer, who for some years now has been trying to find out more about the early life of her late mother, Marjorie. It's a long story, which I will do my best to simplify without causing too much confusion! Although no birth certificate was ever found for Marjorie, she believed she was born in Derby c. 1924, and was associated with the Chinese Quan Sing family, shopkeepers who moved from Derby to Carnarvon in the 1920s. Marjorie was always reluctant to discuss her childhood with her own family, and her daughters believe she may have spent time in an orphanage, as this was hinted at.

It should be added here that Jennifer had only learned about the orphanage reference, just before this time. Discussion had come up at a family gathering and her sister Dawn had mentioned their Mum once hinting to her she had spent time in some sort of care. Jennifer had not known about this, when she was looking for information earlier.

They also think it may be possible that she was illegitimate, and sadly felt ashamed about this, as the topic of her childhood upset her. She was never pushed to talk more about her early life than she was comfortable with, but did reveal memories consistent with her having lived in Carnarvon, with the Quan Sings. We have since met members of the present generation of this lovely family, who believe Marj must be related. This is based on her appearance in photographs, and the accuracy of her memories. Frustratingly, the older folk are no longer with us and when they were asked (by Jennifer) about Marj in the 1980s claimed to have no knowledge of her. Jennifer felt there may have been things left unsaid.

We are also confident that Marj attended a hostel for country girls, Lawley Ladies' College, Mt Lawley, in her teens, as her children remember the college principals (the Misses Sharp) visiting their family in the early 1960s and Marj told her family she would travel home to Carnarvon from Perth by seaplane in school holidays.

Last year we gave Jennifer a DNA test kit as an early 60th birthday present, in the hope it might shed more light on her maternal family line. Her results showed 21 per cent Asia East, and a strong match with one of the Quan Sing descendants, strengthening the belief that a member of that family was one of Marj's parents. This may have been one of the Quan Sing

> sons, or possibly even daughter Yuanho (Una) Quan Sing (b. 1896), who appears to have been quite progressive.
>
> Believed to have been educated at Methodist Ladies' College, she later managed the Derby store and it is documented that she was active in seeking permission to employ Aboriginal workers. Yuanho also moved to Carnarvon with the family; she never married and died in 1959.
>
> Jennifer's test also came back as 62 per cent Europe, which fits her father's England/Ireland lines. No surprises there. It also produced a result of 13 per cent Melanesian, hence this message to you. Your match suggests that you may be a fourth to sixth cousin equivalent with Jennifer, and we're wondering whether there may possibly be a link through you to Marj's unknown parent.
>
> With so many vagaries, it's hard to know how best to phrase useful questions! As a start, we're wondering whether you know of any of your ancestors who may have lived in the Derby area in the early 1920s, or whether any were associated with the Quan Sing family there.
>
> Jennifer is not seeking anything other than information about her mother's history; she says it is as though the first 22 years of Marj's life are a blank canvas.

I thanked Munya for reading so far and added my email address if she would like to make contact. It was a vast amount of information to suddenly dump on someone … but Munya's very upbeat response came in within a couple of days.

> Hello Cheryl, What a delight to hear from you! I am so amazed and excited about my DNA journey. I am finding relatives all

> over the world. I found out I'm related to American actress Kirsty Alley!! Anyway I am only too happy to help Jennifer out in any way I can....

She asked for Marjorie's full name, whether there was a birth certificate and also for copies of any photographs. She would ask some of the older people, if they recognised her. Munya was keen to try to find out her connection with Jennifer, wondering whether it was along Aboriginal lines or through her white father.

> In any event, I am keen to find out and will help out in any way I can. There was an orphanage in Broome run by the Catholic nuns who run the Broome Heritage Centre and they have a huge photo collection of Aboriginal families in the Kimberley. I can also make some enquiries on Jennifer's behalf it you like. Talk to you soon.

On 18 February, we sent off a bundle of photographs and a copy of Marj and Henry York's marriage certificate. Munya responded the same day.

> My first response on seeing the name Dantau is that it may in fact be D'Antoine. He was a Frenchman who married a Bardi woman and they are a well known Kimberley family.
>
> I am in fact related to the D'Antoines, which may account for my being related to Marjorie and her daughter through the Melanesian line rather than my white father. In fact, one of the D'Antoine lads recently contacted me through Ancestry.com as we were matched though our DNA.

Later that year, more information came in from Munya about the D'Antoines.

> Just to add some info about the D'Antoine family. The Aboriginal

> family surname is Hunter, who are my relatives. He was married to Nellie Hunter.

We now know that three of Frenchy D'Antoine's children were Thomas (1890-1984), Annie (1896-1960) and Richard Robert (1900-1967). The sons Thomas and Richard each married Hunter sisters. Thomas married Nellie Hunter (1890-1974) and Richard married her sister, Amy. The Hunter women were the daughters of Harry Hunter whose complex life is well documented in other references.

The same night, Munya shared the following thoughts about her likely connection with Jennifer.

> Hi Cheryl,
>
> Well I've started asking some questions of the D'Antoine family and am waiting a reply.
>
> In the meantime, I've been doing some research.
>
> It's possible Marjory may be a younger sister of Uncle Doug (Douglas Paul D'Antoine) who was born on Bardi country in 1922, some two years before.
>
> His father's name was Thomas D'Antoine and his mother was Nellie Clara Hunter (my relative). His grandfather was Adrian Julius D'Antoine from the Seychelles.
>
> I really think this is the best lead as it would account for the Bardi DNA. As I have no Chinese ancestry it can't be through the Quan Sing line so it has to be through the Aboriginal one.
>
> Hopefully we can unravel this mystery together. How is Jennifer going with all this?
>
> Cheers,
>
> Munya

Attached to the email was an Aboriginal oral history from the WA Museum about Doug D'Antoine and his involvement in the shipbuilding industry.

There was also a family tree diagram showing the family of Thomas D'Antoine and Nellie Hunter. This information was useful, in that it gave us a probable name for Marj's mother. Annie D'Antoine seemed a lot more solid than any of the guesses we'd managed to come up with, after studying the names shown on the 1948 marriage certificate. But we were unable to move the search forward, as other life events, in 2017, saw the year turn to mud.

On 23 January 2018, I sent the next update off to Munya, with greetings for the New Year.

> I hope your DNA story is continuing to unfold.....We had a small development in the past year in that one of Jennifer's second cousins on her Dad's York side had a DNA test. At this point he is her best match. This is proving quite useful as we know that any shared matches between Jennifer and this York cousin must be from her paternal line. At least it helps with the eliminations!
>
> Jennifer is also planning to meet with the Quan Sing family over the Chinese New Year, armed with a DNA kit for one of the family, who have been especially welcoming. She already has one match (3rd to 4th cousin, W.D. Schulze) with a known Quan Sing descendant. And only this week another (more distant) match popped up who shares DNA with W.D. Schulze and with Jennifer.
>
> This new match was with a granddaughter of Lanky's sister, Suju. The amount of shared DNA predicted a 69 per cent probability that Jennifer and her new match were second cousins

> or equivalent. This also fitted the case where Lanky was Marj's father. The name of the mother of this new match was Josephine Constance Kirk, born in Derby in 1927, who had died in New South Wales in 1970. Could this be the 'Josephine (dead)' listed among the information Marj had mentioned to Jennifer? And if so, how had she known?
>
> The results still indicate that there are no other shared matches common to your DNA and Jennifer's, which makes you still very much of interest, particularly as you were born in Derby, as was Marjorie – albeit decades apart.

I also mentioned that Jennifer had found her Mum's old copy of *The Golden Wattle Cookery Book*, with an inscription suggesting it had been given to her about 1940 by Sister Una Florence Ulrich, adding more details about Mrs Ulrich's career and life in the hope that her name might be familiar.

13

REUNION

– JD –

'This could be it,' I kept thinking, over and over, as Geoff was driving me to the airport to catch a mid-morning flight to Broome. It was Sunday, 17 June 2018, a typical sunny Perth winter's day and all I could do was cry.

Geoff was very supportive, saying how glad he was that I'd found my Mum. I guess it was just that the drive to the airport made everything that had happened suddenly seem real. I was very excited, happy and sad, all at once. The whole range of emotions hit me. After thirty-seven years of finding virtually nothing, in a few short weeks, there had been such an overwhelming flood of information.

Mum was with me, I should add. Taking her ashes back to her birth family, on the country she had known as a child, was the whole point. All of my friends had said and James had reminded me on a number of occasions, 'Whatever you do, don't forget your Mother!'

I was also so excited and nervous about meeting Mum's family. Still getting my head around the fact that the people I would soon meet were my family, too.

On Sunday, 27 May, I had made the calls to speak to Mum's nieces Margaret and Dorothy whose late mother Maggie had been Mum's half-sister. They were both so excited. I'd waited until the Sunday afternoon before ringing because I needed to come down a bit from the emotional high I'd been on. I had needed time to gather my thoughts, these were some of the most important calls that I would ever make in my life. Later, I learned that they had been really worried that I wouldn't call them.

By this stage, both ladies knew my name. When I called Margaret, and said 'Hi, my name is Jennifer', she immediately started crying.

'We've been looking for Marjorie, for so long, we can't believe this is happening. Mum made us swear that we would keep looking, as she had done all her life.'

I'd been so calm then, hearing this, talking on the phone.

It was only on the way to the airport that it hit me, right between the eyes. On the flight, I was still emotional and so glad that no-one was sitting next to me. It meant I didn't have to talk to anyone. Puffy, red eyes are not such a great look.

Mum's ashes were in my hand luggage in the overhead locker. They were the first item I'd packed. I thought all over again how heavy they were. Because I wasn't sure what the protocol was for transporting ashes, I'd called a friend who's a travel agent to find out. She'd advised me to find the Certificate of Cremation and carry it with me, just in case there was a problem. As it was, I'd not had to explain anything, my hand luggage had passed through the scanner without a hitch.

Also in my hand luggage was my old blue Bowater Reporter notebook that I'd bought way back in 1981 when the serious part of this search had begun. As well as all my earlier research, it contained a list of questions that I hoped might be answered in the next few days.

Over the course of the two and a half-hour flight, my anxiety slowly began to dissipate. I'd been to Broome several times before including my fiftieth birthday, when Geoff had treated me to a special present. It was a pearl necklace and I wear it all the time. Geoff and I designed it together. The further the plane got away from Perth, and all the emotional turmoil that had happened, the better I felt. By the time we landed at Broome, I felt comfortable, almost like I was coming home.

My mood lifted further when I went to pick up the hire car. I'd booked the smallest, cheapest vehicle I could find, one of those 'lacky band engine' hatchbacks. You can imagine how delighted I was to discover I'd been upgraded to a brand new Toyota RAV4. Thirty-six kilometres on the clock. I was just so glad to be driving a small SUV, something higher off the ground than the small car I'd booked. It was a good start, hopefully a good omen for whatever the next few days held for me.

The KSGAC had booked me into the Broome Time Resort, self-catering accommodation close to Cable Beach. The organisation paid for three days of my stay and I had covered the cost of extending it, mainly because I wanted to get my act together, before and after whatever was about to happen.

Because it was Sunday, James had asked me to call and leave a message on his office answering machine letting him know I'd arrived. I did this after shopping for a few food supplies, driving to Cable

Beach for a brief look around, then returning to the hotel for a quick swim.

It was late afternoon when I left the message, 'Hi James. It's Jennifer … I've arrived safely, and Mum is with me.'

Then I got ready for the sunset, had fish and chips, came back to my room and relaxed. By this stage, I was in a far better place emotionally. James had already arranged for us to meet the following day to discuss a few things, before the big meeting with Margaret and Dorothy scheduled for Wednesday.

On Monday morning, I went for a walk along Cable Beach and met two beautiful Golden Retrievers. I asked the owner why no-one was swimming. 'The locals think the water temperature is too cold,' she told me. I just laughed. It seemed perfect, to me.

Then I went back to my room and had a good breakfast, ready to meet James at the KSGAC office at 10am. I found the office, on Barker Street, quite easily. With its wide verandahs, garden and shade sails, it looked very welcoming, as were all the staff in that busy office when I walked inside. People were coming and going all the time. They all seemed so pleased to have found Mum, James especially. Apparently, her case had been on their books for years. James is a very tall, solid chap and such a tower of strength. He cut quite a colourful figure in the KSGAC uniform. It includes a bright, tropical floral shirt, the feature item being the native hibiscus. The flower is recognised as a national symbol of the Stolen Generation due to its ability to survive and thrive against adversity.

At this meeting, it was mentioned that NAIDOC Week was coming up the following month. This annual event celebrates the history, culture and achievements of Aboriginal and Torres Strait Islander peoples. Every year has a different theme. At some point, I was asked, if I was aware of the theme for 2018? I wasn't. The theme that year was Because of Her, We Can!

That was another OMG moment for me. It was as though I was being sucked up into a big swirling vortex. I cannot stress enough how emotional I felt about the spirituality of all that was happening. It is probably fair to say that by this point, emotionally, I was quite shattered. There were a lot of highs and lows coming at me out of nowhere. Forces seemed to be at work that were way beyond my control.

We had a cup of tea and went through a few things including a family photograph of Mum when she was about five years old. She was with her mother, my grandmother Annie and three of Annie's other children Billy, Joey and Maggie. It was the first photograph I'd ever seen of my mother as a child. Up until then, the youngest photograph of Mum I'd seen was when she was in her twenties. I did not recognise the little girl standing there with her family surrounding her, but I did notice similarities with faces of some of Mum's descendants. Flashes of my nieces Aleisha and Jessine, for instance, my sister Dawn and maybe even a glimpse of me at the same age.

Some of the information the KSGAC had didn't seem to add up. For example, I was asked about Mum having gone to South Australia. I'd heard nothing about South Australia, not even from all the new information that had so recently come in. Glenis Ayling's research had found that Lanky's sister Ena, had married a Frank William Griggs in Adelaide, where their daughter Iris had been born. Frank Griggs and Ena had both died in Adelaide. Maybe, some of the information about Ena had somehow become mixed up with Mum's story. I was starting to realise that the ladies seemed to have had as little information to work with as I'd had. James then asked if

I'd ever heard anything about Mum having gone to Carnarvon with the Aylings. I told him no. So that didn't add up either. From other comments made at that meeting I formed the impression that Mum had been very independent as a girl.

Mum's funeral was planned for Thursday at One Arm Point. On Friday, we were going to Derby where Mum was born.

Over the next few days, I was hoping to find more answers to so many questions. I needed to be careful about getting the facts right about the part of her life we'd missed. When I got home, I wanted to make up fact sheets and family charts and load information on to a USB, to share with Mum's descendants.

Tuesday was a lay day, preparing myself for the next two days. James had suggested, I might like to put a few words together to say at Mum's funeral. So I spent some time going through my notes and trying to relax. I guess the stress must have been starting to tell again. Inside I felt like a coiled spring. So I booked an hour-long back massage. It really hurt! The young German masseur told me afterwards that my tense muscles had made his hands hurt.

I had also tried to call Margaret and Dorothy's brother Frank Davey at One Arm Point and left two messages. I didn't know it then, but Frank was flat out organising Mum's funeral. He must have been rushed off his feet.

James called too, to check how I was. He told me that Dorothy was planning to drive back to One Arm Point on Wednesday night, to be there to greet Mum and me. I thought this was such a kind and respectful act, driving over all that unsealed road, so we would have one familiar face waiting to meet us. He also told me, 'Thursday is getting bigger.' I said it was starting to feel like I would be bringing home the prodigal daughter/sister.

On Wednesday morning, I woke early thinking about Mum, her life and how this had all started. And the big question among so many questions, after all my years of searching, was I about to find out what I wanted to know about Mum? In the back of my mind, I was still anxious that maybe this would all turn out to be a big misunderstanding.

Had I really found Mum?

I was also wondering about this first meeting. What would it be like? I had no idea what to expect. I was so nervous that I kept trying to deflect my thoughts elsewhere, but they just kept coming back to the start. Soon I was packing up, ready to head off to meet Margaret and Dorothy. I double-checked my bag, making sure the photograph album that I'd prepared for them was safe inside. It contained photographs of Mum from around the time of her engagement to Dad and afterwards, throughout her life. There were pictures of Mum arriving at the church as a young bride, then all the York babies in prams. There was Mum with us kids at the Perth Royal Show and lined up to show off a new family station wagon, Mum with fish she'd caught when she and Dad had taken the caravan up near Exmouth, right into her senior years. I really hoped the family would like the gift, and that it would give them a sense of the life Mum had lived.

Margaret and Dorothy were waiting for me when I arrived at the KSGAC. James and the staff had gone to a lot of trouble to put on a wonderful high tea. A table had been set up outside in the shade and they'd thought of everything. There was even a box of tissues. Also there was a man I recognised from my meeting with James earlier in the week. David Cox was there as my support person and was the KSGAC's senior counsellor.

Dorothy is about my age and I also knew that Margaret who was always a little coy about revealing her age was 10 years my senior. Margaret was just so, so happy to see me. She was so overwhelmed, she immediately started crying. Soon we were all teary. The other thing Margaret did was to reach out and take my arm. She just hung on, like she couldn't believe I was real, like she was frightened I might disappear if she let go.

We were all a little bit shy with each other at first, but that didn't last long and soon the conversation became easy. We ended up talking for a couple of hours. There was such a lot to catch up on. They'd started calling me sister straight up, as soon as we'd met. I noticed that Dorothy was the quieter of the two and Margaret kept trying to talk over her like a typical big sister. I guess she was just so emotional and excited. We all were. None of us seemed quite able to believe that this reunion was finally happening.

By this time, I'd accessed Mum's file, but had only had the chance to skim quickly through it. I was at least able to provide a few details like that Mum had won prizes at the Perth Royal Show for her handwriting and needlework. I also knew that Mum had been given the surname King by A.O. Neville, as she came from King Sound and asked what her surname might have been before this. The ladies told me that if Mum did have a surname, it would have been D'Antoine.

They did not know she had been given the name King. If they'd had the new surname, they might have had a better chance of finding her, through the help of the KSGAC, through a records search. They said Mum was born in Derby, and straight after her birth, Annie had moved to Sunday Island. Apparently, Annie had nothing to do with the Quan Sing man after Mum's birth. That saddened me, because from the reports I'd had, Lanky Quan Sing had been a kind and generous person.

On Sunday Island, Mum had enjoyed the freedom of an island childhood, living off the abundance of fruit and vegetables grown there, attending school in the morning and playing all afternoon. Much of the play revolved around the water, which is when the shark-bite story came up. It was believed to have happened when Mum was eight or nine, when she was fishing. She had been given the job of looking after the younger children, a responsibility she'd had from a young age. But on the day of the shark bite, she had taken off to go fishing instead. That made perfect sense to me, she was always at home with a fishing line. I would hear the full story from an eye witness, the following day at One Arm Point. I was very keen to hear this firsthand account, having for so long assumed that the shark bite had happened at Carnarvon.

There were different versions of the story about the big question of how Mum came to be 'taken' to live and work at the Derby Native Hospital. One was that, when Mum was a little older, she and Annie had returned to live in Derby where Annie had found work with the Ayling family. It was here that she had been taken by a Mr Street to train with Mrs Ulrich. It was thought that she had attended the state school in Derby at some point before this. Another line of thought was that Mum had been given to the Ayling family for a better life. Her light colouring, being half Chinese, meant she was targeted. Annie too had been considered light-skinned, being half French.

Some of this information seemed so confusing. What did make perfect sense was the news that Mum's family, the people of the Bardi-Jawi language group, are saltwater people and carry the culture from their ancestors, who lived on the surrounding islands and mainland. They look to the sea for food and sustenance. This news sat very comfortably with me, having witnessed how comfortable Mum was when she connected with the ocean. It's how I feel, too.

It was also interesting to hear that there are sets of twins in the family. Mum's nine grandchildren include twins, daughters of my late brother and sister-in-law, Philip and Jan.

Presenting the photograph album brought more overwhelming emotions, from all of us. I was astounded to learn that both Margaret and Dorothy recognised the photograph of Mum as a bride arriving at the church on the arm of the man, who we had so far failed to identify. And even more surprised to find out that Mum had sent it to them! It turned out Mum had regularly sent parcels, containing handmade children's clothes, biscuits, boiled lollies, knitted jumpers and letters. Annie would read Mum's letters to the other children.

She had also carried a photograph of Mum on her wedding day. It was with her always, used as a bookmark in Annie's Bible. Later, I would hear the comment, 'We always had the best toys at Christmas. The girls had the best dolls on Sunday Island.'

It is thought that a Sunday Island missionary, a Mr Holmes, had been the link between Mum's correspondence and her birth family. I was also a little shocked to hear that none of Mum's letters and parcels had ever contained a return address. Why? When she had so obviously gone to so much trouble to send them?

I had no knowledge that Mum had sent these parcels. But this new information brought to mind Mum's fortnightly food shopping trips when I was a child. When Dad would rush home at lunchtime to pick up Mum and her covered shopping trolley on wheels and drive her back to Midland. He would leave her to shop for groceries, go to the butcher, the bank and the post office. Had the hampers, destined for her family on Sunday Island, been inside that trolley?

The line of communication had stopped in 1964, when the Sunday Island Mission closed. Some of the Sunday Islanders had moved to Beagle Bay, others to Lombardina and eventually, some had regrouped later at Ardyaloon where the One Arm Point community now stands. I was even more shocked to learn that the island people had been left to fend for themselves on the beach.

I also wondered what Mum had written about in those letters. Did she mention us kids? If there was no return address, was she also careful in what she wrote? Was she worried about letting on where she was living? The ladies told me Mum's letters and gifts had been treasured and kept. Then, after the islander people had been relocated to the mainland, a truck, containing those treasures, had been stolen. Their last links with Mum, their daughter and sister, had been taken from them. Margaret and Dorothy also presented me with a copy of the photograph of Mum as a five-year-old.

By the time our afternoon tea came to an end, I was full with new information. There was such a lot to process. I'd also learned that the next day's reunion for Mum would no longer be just a quiet spreading of ashes as I had assumed. A full, coming-home funeral service had been planned. The scale of it was news to me, and I was very glad I'd prepared something to say. 'Two funerals – who on earth gets two funerals?'

The next day was Thursday, 21 June 2018. I was awake at 4.30am. For some reason, I couldn't really sleep. Funny that. Mum's ashes were packed in my carry-on bag, right by the door. James and David picked me up before 8.00am, as we were due at One Arm Point around mid-morning. We stopped to pick up Margaret on our way. Dorothy had gone on ahead to be part of the greeting party.

In no time at all, we were zooming north towards the Dampier Peninsula. One Arm Point is the northernmost community on the Cape Leveque Road, described as an Aboriginal Australian community town that, at the 2016 census, had a population of 365. At the time of my visit, it was generally known as One Arm Point, or the Bardi community. (The name has since changed to Ardyaloon, as it is considered more appropriate.)

The unsealed Pindan took about two hours to cover. (Much of the road we travelled is sealed now, I think the unsealed section can be covered in around 17 minutes.) It was a bone- jarring experience. At the end of it, I considered myself lucky that I still had my kidneys!

When we drove into One Arm Point, the housing, the streets, the airport and all the surroundings reminded me so much of Broome. Red soil, white beaches and turquoise ocean.

Our first call was at the home of community Elders Frank and Maureen Davey, Mum's nephew and his lovely wife. By this time, Frank and I had spoken on the telephone, a couple of times. When he greeted us, I noticed he'd put on a red shirt just for Mum and me. He'd heard that red was Mum's favourite colour and mine too and, while I suspect he would usually have worn black at a funeral like this, he'd honoured us in this way. I found this immensely moving. He considered my Mum important enough to break with this tradition.

Margaret was the keeper of the photograph album, at this stage, and shared it with Frank. His reaction, when he saw Mum's wedding photograph, amazed me. 'That's the photo we had,' he said. 'That's Mr Holmes!' I would later learn that the missionary on Sunday Island who'd been the link between Mum and her family was thought to have been Will Holmes. Frank remembered that he had a distinctive cleft in his chin, just like the man in the wedding photograph.

After a gathering at Frank's house to welcome me as Mum's daughter, we all moved to the Cemetery for Mum's burial.

The school had been closed for the day, in honour of Mum's return home and an order of service booklet had been produced with the heading Special Burial Ceremony for Marjorie. Quite a crowd had started to gather. I was beginning to understand why Frank had been so hard to contact in the past couple of days.

The site looked out over the top end of King Sound, towards Sunday Island, where the water is that beautiful colour that I can only describe as Broome blue. It is one of the group of islands known as the Buccaneer Archipelago, famous for its white sandy beaches. It was there that Mum had enjoyed the sort of idyllic freedom, which kids today can only dream about, if they're given the freedom to dream. The site also looked towards the point at the end of a huge bay, a landmark that Frank described as Mum's point. I couldn't think of anywhere else in the world as a more appropriate final resting place for her.

Mum's grave had already been dug, in a spot close to the graves of her sisters Dolly and Maggie. I learned from their memorial plaques that Dolly was 10 years older than Mum and had passed away in 2001, Maggie had been just four years older than Mum and had passed away in 2004. It was their searching that had inspired Margaret, Dorothy and Frank to never give up.

At what I now think of as Mum's first funeral, I'd delivered the eulogy and the only way I could manage that was by stepping outside of myself, an out-of-body experience. At this second funeral, hanging on to the jarrah box containing Mum's ashes, I was able to go with the flow a little better, though there were still a few teary moments.

David Cox who is also a minister of religion opened the service with a prayer, then Frank addressed the family on the search for Marjorie. He also shared the story of her childhood encounter with the shark, at Sunday Island. Apparently, Mum's shark encounter had become a local legend.

Then it was my turn to describe my search and my journey towards reunion. I put the box containing Mum's ashes on a table that had been set up specially. It had a red tablecloth, and floral arrangements of gerberas and red roses stood at either end. Mum would have loved that, she was always a keen gardener.

I told the assembled crowd that my serious search had started, when I was about 23 years of age.

'I had always asked Mum questions, but had no real answers in return.

'Mum would rarely speak about her early days, and when she did she always broke down and cried. It was too painful for her to talk about.'

I shared the few clues she had given me, about her belief that Lanky Quan Sing was her father, the shark bite, her love of fishing, a piece of tin being thrown into her eye, that she was born in Derby but at some point had ended up in Carnarvon.

Then I described how, after years of nothing, a friend of a friend had mentioned my quest, which led to my contact with Julie QuanSing-Rowlands. We'd each had a DNA test and my Quan Sing connection had been verified.

But I still had nothing at all about Mum's mother.

I went on to describe how everything had changed so suddenly, after discovering Mrs Ulrich's staff file where a Marjory King was mentioned. Although I still was not sure if this Marjory was my mother, I had applied to the state government for the file.

'Five days later, and completely unrelated to my request for the file, Julie had forwarded an email from her nephew, who had forwarded her an email, sent to him by James Feehan, of the Kimberley Stolen Generation Aboriginal Corporation. People in the Kimberley were looking for their relative. There was a connection with Derby, Carnarvon and a family called Quan Sing.

'After a few more telephone calls and emails, James was able to confirm that my Mum was, in fact, the sister whose family had been searching for her. We had all been searching, for such a long time.

'I found this so hard to believe, and still do. After so many years of nothing, suddenly in the space of five days, we had made the connection that would answer so many questions. For both sides of Mum's family.'

Briefly, I filled in some gaps telling how Mum had stayed in Derby with Mrs Ulrich and others, working at the hospital for about four years. She had then been given an opportunity to work for a family who were moving to Carnarvon where she stayed for just one year.

She had then had the chance to move to Perth to train at Lawley Ladies' College. She had trained in dressmaking and also nursing, which had led to her working as a nursing aide at the Mount Hospital in Perth. It was there that she'd met my father.

'After they married, on 10 April 1948, they made their home in the Swan Valley, and raised four children. Mum's life seemed to be happy – fishing, raising the kids, going to the footy, being part of the community and loving her family. We were lucky to have such a loving mother, who looked after us. Even though we may not have had a lot of material things, we always had plenty of food. We never went hungry. As a child I can remember lots of fishing, crabbing and swimming. Something we all still do now.'

I told them how Mum had simply got on with her life after Dad died, passing her driving test, travelling all over Australia, and easily making new friends. She also just loved to sing, joke and enjoy herself. Also, that she had loved nothing more than her children, nine grandchildren and at the time of her passing, two little great-grandchildren. Despite being in a lot of pain, towards the end of her life, her face would always beam when she saw the little ones.

'I believe that Mum had a full life, surrounded by love, and we are all richer for having shared some part of it.

'Thank you to everyone involved in all of this. For all of us, not giving up. It is impossible to express how I truly feel. At last, so many questions have been answered, and now I can have closure.

'Thank you all, for bringing Mum home.'

It still seems incredible that I could cover so much ground in a short speech like that. But I reckoned the people who remembered Mum and had invested so much in the search for her deserved to have some of their questions answered too.

James then spoke about the background to the search after he'd started with the KSGAC as a caseworker and had taken a new approach in a cold-case review.

David then did a bible reading, before the formal burial proceedings began. I passed Mum's box of ashes to one of the two younger men, who'd been chosen as pallbearers for this very reverent burial and gave the box one final pat before it was placed in the base of the grave.

Then, I led the family in placing a handful of sand on the casket before the hymn 'God be with you till we meet again' and closing prayers. After the grave was filled, raked, levelled and surrounded by smooth white rocks, we lined up to put fresh, long-stemmed red roses into the sand.

Among the guests at Mum's funeral was respected Elder Bessie Ejai, who has done an enormous amount of work helping to educate the local children about their culture, the Bardi language and how to look after their country. She is about six years younger than Mum, and I'd been so looking forward to meeting her.

Bessie was the only person I'd ever met who knew Mum as a child. She is the little girl who witnessed the shark attack. She was at the beach and was able to tell all of us, assembled by Mum's grave, what she remembered of the event. She said Mum had cast a hand line into the water and had hooked a fish. The problem was, a black-tip shark had its eyes on the fish, too! Whether or not Mum saw the shark is not known. But having seen how determined she was when fishing with us kids off the coast near Perth, I can believe she would have been capable of standing her ground, even with a shark in the water.

She had reeled in the fish and had it up and out of the water, when bang! The shark made its grab for the fish, missed it, but shot forward with its jaws wide open, latching on to Mum's knee instead. That explained the shark jaw-shaped silver scars that had marked Mum for life. I'd been waiting all my life to hear that story and am so grateful that Bessie was able to tell it.

Frank said Mum's injury would probably have been treated with a combination of traditional and western medicine. I thought back to those poultices Mum used to make using bread, onions, sugar and soap and had to wonder whether a similar treatment had been used on her bite.

Then we moved down to Middle Beach where the community school pupils had made a Welcome Home banner and did a song presentation. Some of the children were sugar-coated with beach sand, even on their faces. Seeing them reminded me of our family trips to the beach when I was young, when I'd spin over and over rolling through the sand, until I looked like I was coated in sugar.

Frank presented me with two shells, a bracelet and a cap, gifts from this special part of his world, for me to take back home to mine. Then I was taken to the historic Round Rock Lookout with its spectacular views. I was amazed at how quickly the water was swirling past and could appreciate why the area is so famous for its racing tides.

After lunch, the world-famous Bardi dancers performed *Ilma*, while Frank explained to me the Dreamtime story that the dance was telling. *Ilma* is the Bardi word for corroboree and is also the name of the handheld dance apparel that is used to help explain the meaning of the dance. Among the performers was Frank and Maureen's son Moochoo. This traditional dance troupe has performed all around the world, sharing through dance the stories of their ancient culture. In 2006, they performed at Stonehenge, the only Aboriginal dance troupe ever to do so.

Frank then took us to the Trochus Hatchery and Aquaculture Centre, located right on the tip of the Dampier Peninsula. This is the only hatchery of its kind in Australia and was set up, to address the problem of declining trochus shell numbers in the wild. I learned that the trochus, a type of sea snail, is valued by the local community as a food source. The inner mother-of-pearl shell is also used to make jewellery and buttons. One of the markets is Europe where trochus shells are used for high-end fashion. The hatchery also grows sea turtles, coral and all sorts of fish including barramundi and clown fish.

Later, when talking to Maureen about Mum's love of fishing, I learned that to the Bardi-Jawi people, parts of the fish including the roe are considered special eating. That took me back to eating freshly caught fish when I was growing up, where Mum had always considered the fish roe such a delicacy.

Frank then took us to what he calls The Block, the Gumbanan Wilderness Retreat, the Davey family's tourist operation. They set up the retreat, to raise awareness about the Bardi culture and its connection with the sea and the land.

Culture is everything to Frank. He lives and breathes it. He told me that he'd realised, years ago, that he needed to get a good education in order to be able to help his people. As well as being the Bardi dance troupe leader, he's a mover and shaker in so many other fields – the Kimberley Land Council, Kimberley Aboriginal Caring For Culture Progam and the Bardi Ranger Program -- where Elders are taken out on country to provide advice and children are educated about their language and culture. These are just a few.

I also found out that Mum had spoken Bardi. This was a surprise to me, having been told by her that she had spoken Chinese as a child. I have since learned that the v sound does not occur in Bardi. That explained why Mum had always had trouble pronouncing vegetables and the name Viskovich.

I was also told that day Mum's name was Ngarrdab, then I was given the honour of my own name Joondub, after my great-grandmother Nundra.

One of the immediate family presented me with a big framed photograph of Mum and a visiting family gave me a fresh pearl shell, picked just that morning.

It had been a big day. I was so privileged to have this sharing time to make so many connections. It was like the whole town had turned up. There was even the chance to meet AJ, my new DNA match.

(Just a few weeks before, I would not have believed this would have been possible.) But when Mum's second funeral was over, the team at KSGAC had not quite finished with me yet.

On Friday, they took the corporation's bus out for a good run, with Dorothy and me on board, heading to Derby. As mentioned earlier, a long bus ride is a wonderful place for a deep conversation. I found myself sneaking little sideways glances at Dorothy, she was sneaking glances at me too. And sometimes, our glances would connect. So much about Dorothy reminded me of Mum. Her high forehead, maybe a slight hand movement. Her smile. When she tilted her head a certain way, I would catch a glance of Mum in her face.

I still can't get over how emotional it was experiencing this. But it was all good. It was great, actually.

My impression of Derby itself was unsettling. After the pristine beauty that Mum had known on Sunday Island, I knew she would have hated the place described in the letters Mrs Ulrich had written.

One of the main purposes of this trip was to allow me to meet members of the D'Antoine family. My connections through Mum's grandfather Frenchy. There was a big turnout in the shade at a local park.

The first surprise was to meet someone else who remembered Mum when she was young. No-one for sixty-one years, now two people in two days! Peggy D'Antoine had visited Mum when she had worked at Derby Native Hospital. She told me she'd been allowed to visit because her colouring was considered quite light.

Again, I heard the version of the story about how Annie had taken Mum with her, when she moved from Sunday Island to Derby to work for the Ayling family. One day, when Annie was out, Mum had been taken by a missionary Mr Street and handed over to Mrs Ulrich at the hospital. Mum had apparently attended school in Derby but continued school by correspondence while at the hospital.

Some of this matched what I knew, but some of the information was still at odds with what had been found out through other sources. The opinion of the D'Antoine family was that Mum looked a lot like her sister Dolly as she got older and also like her mother Annie.

Annie was also very shy and quiet and softly spoken, a bit like Mum had been until she got to know people. It surprised me to hear that Annie had seen Mum for the last time when she was working at Derby Native Hospital. I wondered then, if the story about wanting a better life for Mum might have an element of truth. I hoped so. And it was some comfort to know that Annie had maintained some sort of connection. She'd seen the photograph of Mum on her wedding day. I hoped she was able to be happy for her.

In the past few days, I had entered an enormous amount of information in my blue notebook. Looking at the cover, I realised, that a more accurate description of the cover's colour is Broome blue.

At that point, I knew I was now done. Mum had been returned to country. Her family had found her. I now knew how she had lived, before she was taken. And fishing was her first love. That made perfect sense.

We are saltwater people of the Bardi-Jawi culture.

And I am Joondub.

A saltwater woman.

14

THE LAST WORD

– CR –

In 1975, when Una F. Ulrich had stayed with the Yorks at West Swan and shared a room with Jennifer, she had presented her with a Bible as a thank-you gift. Inside, on the fly leaf, she had written her thanks for sharing and added a reference to a passage from the New Testament, Acts 17:26. Jennifer was seventeen when she received this gift and I was a year older. It is fair to say that our knowledge of the Bible was not at the top of the list of our potential *Mastermind* subjects, and nor would it be today. But we had a stab. Without the benefit of the internet, the best we came up with, in that clumsy attempt, was 'it must mean something about sharing'.

Forty-five years on, the subject of that Bible came up again. It seemed like a good idea to make another attempt at a meaningful translation. This time, we turned to sources likely to have a few more clues

Jennifer posed the question to her work colleague Claudine, who took it to a higher authority on religion and forwarded this response the following day,

> Acts 17:26 – King James Version: And hath made of one blood all nations of men for to dwell on all the face of the earth, and hath determined the times before appointed, and the bounds of their habitation.

The interpretation included the following comments,

> All will be equal in flesh and blood. Nobody is to look down on another or think that they or their family is above others.
>
> Regardless of race, religion, nations, all will be on earth, some in different countries, tribes etc.
>
> God will decide the time when we are born and depart from this earth, and where we shall live on earth.

Given the context, that Marj was a member of the Stolen Generation, the interpretation had wrapped up with,

> It would seem that the lady who took your Mother under her wing … used this verse to perhaps remind herself that she is not superior to others and she accepts your mother as equal. At that time, it was probably frowned upon to do that.

Or, as Claudine summarised, 'Really, it's about how we are all equal.'

PART TWO

CONNECTIONS

15

THOUGHTS

Whenever Jennifer or Cheryl had a new idea they would email the other, followed by the question, 'Thoughts?' It therefore seems appropriate as the title for their respective points of view.

One: Completing the circle

– CR –

Helping with the story of this remarkable journey has been a privilege. It has also been a rollercoaster ride of emotions, a comment endorsed by so many that this story so far has touched. Julie QuanSing-Rowlands' comment, after reading the draft first seven chapters was,

> … I can't believe what a profound effect this book has had on me so far. So many memories at the personal level … things that remind me of my Mum, life on the plantation, the era as well as world events … I almost feel the life you describe could be my life.

My hope is that others will be moved, too. Moved to laughter, and moved to tears. Moved to speak out when you see something you perceive to be wrong. Moved too, to speak out when you see something you perceive to be *right*.

When events first began to unfold midway through 2018, as a writer I didn't dare touch it. It was way too raw, and it involved so many complex and controversial sensitivities. Besides, other aspects of my own family life were so busy, how could I possibly commit the time and emotional energy to something that would do justice to Marjorie's story? To Marjorie herself?

Two years on, however, there had been a generational and occupational shift. Certain obligations had lifted. I recognised that the true story of Jennifer's journey to unlock the mystery of her mother's past was both captivating and inspirational. Then out of the blue, had come a call from Jennifer, 'Hi. Are you free? I want to talk, all about me!'

She wanted me to help her write this book. She wanted to hold this story in her hands, and to be able to pass it on to Marjorie's descendants and others who might be chasing answers in their own lives.

Soon afterwards, Jennifer and I were talking about the lightning bolt hitting the kitchen fridge, when she was about six years old and living at West Swan. In the split-second after I'd said, 'So….was the fridge damaged?', there was the briefest silence. I could hear it echoing all the way down the telephone line. Like she considered the question a bit thick.

'Yeah … well, what do *you* think! It blew the *arse* out of the fridge.'

It was such a Jennifer thing to say, and caught her writer's voice so perfectly. If this was to be an honest account, then her unique sense of humour had to be part of it. Who else would read *Wuthering Heights,* up the back of a grandstand at a football match, while their mother waved her black and white brolly at her team's opponents?

Telling the story of Jennifer's childhood and her growing realisation about the silence of her Mum's past seemed the perfect pitch for the story of the life Marjorie had led. I knew I could tell you things about Jennifer that she would almost certainly never write about herself.

I took such a logical, checking-the-records approach to the search. It was only near the end, that I'd learned we would never have found the Marjorie King file any earlier because it had not yet been released.

Another challenge has been that several key players shared the same name. Una Quan Sing, Una F. Ulrich and Una Whiteman. Then, there were two Mr Holmes. The missionary Will R. Holmes appears to be unrelated to the Rev. George Holmes, whose family we now know Marjorie had lived with when they were based at the Australian Inland Mission in Carnarvon. From records, it also appears that Will R. Holmes lived out his retirement in Bassendean, an 11-minute walk away from Jennifer and Geoff's house. Just like Miss Mabel Ross 'China' Sharp, he'd lived well within reach and probably held the answers to so many of Jennifer's questions. If only she had known that, back then.

The abundance of family history in my background has highlighted the deafening silence surrounding Marjorie's history. I spent much of my childhood shadowing my maternal grandparents. Jennifer had no idea who or where hers were.

Also, Jennifer had not been clued up to go down any indigenous rabbit holes. Marjorie had been so clever in putting Jennifer off the scent with all her carefully dropped clues, those shreds of baited information containing mere grains of truth. The crumbs she'd dropped had led us right up the garden path, all the way back to her Chinese heritage in Carnarvon.

Then there was that entry in my mother's 1994 diary. Marj and Mum, by that stage, had been friends for forty-six years. I can rationalise why the subject of Carnarvon had come up in their telephone call that day, as a relative had recently moved to Geraldton and had a son in Carnarvon. And Marj's comments as recorded by Mum seemed to make such perfect sense. Marj had said her parents ran a shop in Carnarvon, that her Dad had died in 1954 and her mother when she was ten. It only served to illuminate the signposts back to Carnarvon in a stronger light.

We suspected just about everyone Jennifer had talked to of hiding something from her. When in fact it was Marjorie, the innocent at the centre of this mystery, who had been so adept at feeding out false clues. It pains me to think that Marj had thought it necessary, as recently as 1994, to still be covering her tracks.

Once the decision to present alternating points of view had been made, it became clear that the story of the search to find Marjorie King could also be a platform for other themes it had raised, both negative and positive. Friendship, paternalism, loyalty, prejudice, connection, family secrets, racism, culture, the lost Swan Valley of our childhood, the kindness of strangers, errors of judgement, our sense of identity, the importance of literacy and sharing stories, to name just a few.

In researching some of the experiences of the Stolen Generation, I have stumbled across many stories and images that are deeply moving. The one I think about often, was from the State Library of Western Australia's 2019 photographic exhibition 'From Another View'. This was when I'd been trying to track down one of the two Mr Holmes who had been an influence in Marj's life. This particular Mr Holmes was Will Holmes the missionary believed to have been the link between Marjorie and her birth family on Sunday Island. The person who had delivered her carefully packed parcels. That search had led to a photograph linked to Mt Margaret Mission, south of Laverton.

It showed Mysie and her son Roderick Schenk, who were from a missionary family, and a school inspector standing on the platform of a nearby railway station. With them is a tall Aboriginal man, described in the caption as 'an unknown friend.' A visitor to the exhibition had later identified this unknown man. He was 'Old Man Mr Morgan' who met every train. Looking for his family.

The fate of Agnes Molloy, the little girl who worked at Derby Native Hospital at the same time as Marjorie, both intrigued and worried me. What had become of her? A listing for a grave under that name had shown up online in Collie Shire Cemetery. This Agnes had died in 2001, aged 74, which seemed a good match.

Leanne Old, whom I'd met through our shared interest of Swan Valley family history, lives in Collie. So after exhausting the usual leads I shot off an email to Leanne, wondering whether she remembered Agnes. I asked her not to spend time on this, it would be a yes or no answer. The next day a photograph of the magnificent, polished granite ledger, marking the Agnes Molloy grave, arrived. Leanne had called the cemetery, located the grave and driven out to get a photograph. The wording answered so many questions.

> Agnes was a daughter, sister, Auntie and friend to many.
>
> Tragically taken twice. Taken from her family as a child of Iwanya (Sunday Island) and Dampier Peninsula in the Kimberley.
>
> A beautiful woman and style icon, taken suddenly in 2001, as

an adult, from her adopted families, friends and the community she cherished.

Missed and loved always.

The wording was so carefully chosen. It painted a picture of a beautiful woman, a style icon, someone who'd been loved enough for her life to have been remembered in such a moving tribute.

Marilyn Horner tracked down a South-West funeral director who recalled a modern woman, ahead of her time, who had organised her own prepaid funeral long before this practice became fashionable. While friend Maria Weighell remembered a quiet, gentle woman who was a regular at Collie Baptist Church. 'Agnes had a good sense of humour and was respected by all at our fellowship,' she said.

Pauline Harcourt Quan Sing's story saddened me too. It would have been convenient for us had one of her daughters with Lanky survived. A line of descent known to have stemmed from Lanky Quan Sing might have helped fine-tune Jennifer's genetic connection to him. It might have helped her to say with certainty that Lanky was her grandfather. Rather than probably was.

What was inconvenient for us must have been such tragedy for her. She was a nurse and midwife who spent her working life bringing babies into the world, yet never got to raise her own. As someone for whom motherhood came late and not without earlier disappointment, I found a connection with Pauline and an empathy that completely surprised me. As for general nurse and midwife Sister Una F. Ulrich, all I can do is present the facts as we found them. She spent much of her life delivering health care into communities, often so remote that it was near impossible to attract health professionals to work there. She had worked through drought and the Great Depression. Nor was Una F. Ulrich frightened to have her name in print, to call out blatant racism in a Perth daily newspaper. Many parts of The Ulrich Files make harrowing reading on so many fronts. The language and attitudes of the time are confronting.

It does seem clear that Una F. Ulrich was deeply fond of Marjorie. They were photographed together in Perth, in the weeks before Marjorie and Henry York's 1948 wedding. She was there again in April 1949, for the birth of the York's first baby Philip. Una and Marjorie remained in contact until the end of Una F. Ulrich's life.

Mrs Ulrich had regarded Marjorie as she might have regarded a daughter. But Marjorie already had a mother Annie on Sunday Island. The risk in making too many assumptions is that the circumstances surrounding Marjorie being taken remain unclear. There are conflicting versions of events, as those involved agree.

It does seem clear that the tie between Marj and Annie was not severed completely, as there were letters and hampers until the Sunday Island Mission closed. I hope Annie found some comfort when she saw the happiness reflected in her daughter's face in her wedding photograph. How poignant that she had carried that photograph with her always, kept safe in her Bible.

Many of these people were caught up in the net that was the context of a particular time in Australian history. Marjorie, part Chinese, part Aboriginal and born in 1924 had through an accident of time and place landed in the middle of a perfect storm. From the moment she found herself at Derby Native Hospital, there would be no going back. However, around the age of 21, Marjorie was given a choice. And she ran with it.

The Marjorie York I knew was devoted to her children and grandchildren, loved her home, was a loyal and funny friend and a fierce Swan Districts Football Club supporter. Maybe she considered herself lucky to have found someone who every summer would take one month off work and take her and the children fishing every second day. But she should have been encouraged to share her new life with her birth family too. The laws of the day did not allow her to.

As much as this story contains elements of overwhelming loss, I hope you will also find much to celebrate and many to admire. There are those whose work helps keep culture, history and language alive, from Bessie Ejai, Frank Davey and all of Jennifer's Bardi-Jawi connections passing on their wisdom about the sea and land and knowledge of the Bardi language to a new generation on the Dampier Peninsula to those who continue to speak and teach it.

Not to forget the professional historians, archivists, librarians and amateur enthusiasts, Dr Chris Owen, Chris Jakes, the archivists at the State Records Office in Perth, the late Una Whiteman and Lila Baker, Marilyn Horner and Glenis Ayling, to name a few. And Munya Andrews whose life purpose includes creating a better understanding and appreciation of Aboriginal people.

It is only by preserving our written and oral histories that the current generation will be able to inherit something that might be worth passing on, into the future. Most of all, it is a celebration of the power of curiosity, conversations and connection. There is the connection between land and sea and the importance of the sustainable management of both. Then there is the connection between people that drove this story on towards its conclusion.

When Chad Horner connected with Kirsty Campbell, this meant their respective mothers Marilyn Horner and Verna Campbell also connected. And because Marilyn and Lindsay were co-godparenting our children with Jennifer and Geoff, family-history enthusiast Marilyn had become aware of Jennifer's quest.

It was inevitable that, at some point, Marilyn would share news of the quest with her new in-law Verna whose family were Chinese and had lived in Carnarvon. Had Verna heard of a family called Quan Sing? Not only had Verna heard of the family, she and her husband Bill had remained in contact with a daughter of that big family, Julie QuanSing-Rowlands, after they'd moved to Perth. That was the bridge that had helped Jennifer to connect with Julie in 2013.

Although the Quan Sing connection provided a wealth of information about the Chinese line of Jennifer's ancestry, it had not led to any new information about her mother's maternal line. That all changed five years later, in 2018, when a new caseworker took a fresh approach to a cold case being investigated by the Kimberley Stolen Generation Aboriginal Corporation. The case involved a young woman called Marjorie.

Caseworker James Feehan made a pitch to Jeremy Quan Sing. He had evidence of a Quan Sing connection with Marjorie.

Perhaps the most touching part of this story is the knowledge that for all the years that Jennifer was searching, her mother's birth family was searching too. Way up north on the Dampier Peninsula, a light had never stopped burning. A family was waiting for their saltwater girl to come home.

Two: We were never alone

– JD –

For a long time, I have believed that there is something out there that's bigger than we are. And also, that events happen when they are meant to, when the stars line up. I guess this must be the spiritual side of me coming out, just like Mum.

Take the night when Geoff and I met at that party when I'd dived in through the window of his car. We later discovered that we'd been moving in similar circles for years. Mainly through playing cricket out in the Swan Valley, his list of friends and acquaintances overlapped with some of the names on mine. We'd even been at the same cricket club dance held in the hall, just across the road from my old primary school in Caversham, not all that long before we met. I remember another dive under a table up the back of the hall, to drag one of my former teachers out on to the floor for a dance. The teacher was in the same cricket club as Geoff, see what I mean? But for some reason, Geoff and I didn't meet that night. Maybe we weren't quite ready for each other. The time wasn't right for us to connect.

I am just so glad that none of this had come to light in 2012. There is no way I would have coped. If the photograph of Julie QuanSing-Rowlands had been in the newspaper that year, it's likely I wouldn't have had the time to read it. And if someone had drawn it to my attention, it's also highly likely I would have done nothing. There was too much going on.

This is not a whinge, it's simply a statement of fact. Bad stuff happens to most of us. I tend to just suck it up and get on with it. Such a lot of bad stuff happened that year and some of it came all at once. In mid-autumn, Geoff and I had gone to Melbourne knowing that as soon as we got back, I'd be going into hospital to have a hysterectomy. I wasn't even feeling sick, but my surgeon thought it was the best course of action and did not want to delay the surgery.

Just before I went into hospital, my best friend's mother had died. I couldn't go to her funeral because I was in hospital having the operation that day and it took longer than planned, because it was not the simple keyhole surgery that my doctor had hoped it would be. I remember being really upset and angry about not being able to attend that funeral. She had been an important influence in my life, and I had so wanted to honour her.

That was in April and I had six weeks' sick leave afterwards to try to recover. I was still on sick leave when Cheryl's father Harry Rogers passed away. He had also been a big influence when I was growing up and, with his wife Audrey, had been close friends with my Mum. His funeral was on 31 May, by which time I was able to attend, but I wasn't exactly firing on all cylinders.

The one good thing that happened was in September when we picked up our new Jack Russsell puppy Pepper. Geoff chose the name because she was all over everything. Her birth date was 9 July, the fifth anniversary of Mum's passing away. That seemed like a sign to me that she was meant to be with us. She was and still is as cute as. But as anyone who takes on the responsibility of a puppy will tell you, they are also a great deal of work. Puddles, training, more puddles. We were still settling her in, when I got home from work one night and, as Geoff was taking off his boots, he told me he'd been diagnosed that day with throat cancer. That was his big news. Then, I told him mine. 'And I've just lost my job,' I said. 'I've been made redundant.'

It seems hard to believe that we could be struck with two such significant setbacks, all within the space of a day. It was not long before my fifty-fourth birthday. There didn't seem to be much to look forward to. The prospect of finding a new job was particularly daunting. I was unemployed for six weeks with only a couple of interviews, then the Bankwest job had come up. It was such a huge relief when they told me my application had been successful. I started the job on 8 November. The downside was that the work was all new to me and involved weeks and weeks of training, getting used to unfamiliar systems. Sometimes,

I felt like I was drowning.

It is fair to say that my head was not in the best place during this time. One of the worst things was not being able to take Geoff to any of his appointments for treatment, because I was in a new job and I was so angry and resentful about that. I was new and didn't feel that I knew what I was doing. It was a tough time and dented my confidence.

Geoff and I were so grateful that our friends got together and one or the other would be Geoff's taxi, driving him to and from his appointments for medical treatment. This happened every week day, for weeks.

We had been discussing cancelling our income protection policy, just before all this happened, as the premiums were quite steep. Thank God, we didn't. We had never made a claim either. At least, it meant Geoff was able to get some income support, while he was unable to work. It still took a lot of the wind out of our sails financially. It was also a relief to have top hospital and private health cover. That meant we could cover the cost of the chemotherapy and only had a small gap to pay for the radiotherapy treatments.

Between April and December, I'd had to deal with a hysterectomy, the deaths of two people who had both been an enormous influence on my life, redundancy at almost fifty-four, Geoff's cancer treatment, and a challenging new job that I needed to make work. And Pepper. At some point, I basically shut down to cope and got on with it. I had to. I have never considered myself a victim. Mum was the same.

The bottom line is had we not connected with Julie we may never have found Mum. If just one of the links that led me to Mum's birth family had been broken, her story could so easily have slipped away.

By the time the newspaper article about Julie appeared, on May 24 of the following year, I was in a much better place. Although Geoff was still having health issues recovering from his treatments, he'd had all his clearances from his doctors. I had broken through the barrier at work too and felt far more confident in what I was doing. Even Pepper had settled in and her puppy behaviour had improved considerably. She had become a lot easier to manage.

So, when the story about Julie came to my attention, the time seemed right to make a move. I kept following the thread, right up to Mum's second funeral.

I bawled my eyes out when I found out that Mum's family had never given up looking for her. That was such a shock. The open arms of the Bardi-Jawi family and people was unbelievable. They too have closure of their quest to find Mum. We were never alone.

When I got back from Broome, in 2018 and people started hearing about this story, and how all the events had unfolded, so many said I needed to get it written down. The time was not right. I was still processing so much information, much of which had come out of the blue after years of nothing. I was in no state to go public.

My main focus was in privately distributing the information that had come to light, to my sister and brothers and their families. They were the people who'd been closest to Mum and it seemed right that they be informed first. That way, if any of Mum's future descendants has any questions, they should be well positioned to access the answers.

When I got back, I hired a room in a community hall and invited my three siblings, along with their children. My sister Dawn and her daughters were able to attend, as was my brother George and my late brother Philip was represented by his twin girls.

Each line of the family was given a thumb drive, containing information from Mum's personal files, a family tree, a fact sheet and photographs from the album I'd given to her nieces in the Kimberley. I'd also had copies made of the photograph of Mum as a child, which I'd been given, to distribute that day. In the fact sheet, I described some of my journey of discovery and what was now known about Mum's early life. It finished with:

> Earlier this year after making contact with some of the family of Mum's late mother Annie, I travelled to Broome to meet my cousins and learn more about Mum's early history. They were able to tell me that Mum's great love was fishing and also confirmed the story about the shark bite on her knee. I found out that Mum belonged to the Bardi-Jawi people, also known as Salt Water People. This made a lot of sense to me.
>
> I spoke to several elders who remembered Mum and particularly remembered going fishing with her. They all said she was a quiet, helpful and softly spoken girl. Her Aboriginal name is Ngarrdab. And I was given the name Joondub in honour of my great-grandmother Nundra.
>
> Two of Annie's grand-daughters (Mum's half-nieces) had been looking for Mum ever since Annie and their own mother had passed away. They had never given up.
>
> I confirmed with Philip and Dawn that they were happy for me to take Mum's ashes back to her birth mother's family. This was a relief as in 11 years we as a family had never come to a satisfactory conclusion about where Mum's final resting place should be ... and not in my front room.
>
> Mum's family warmly welcomed her return and she is now resting at One Arm Point family cemetery, overlooking the ocean and her Point.

I knew it was a lot for everyone to take in, all at once, but at least they had something to take away and learn from as time allowed. I also made a short speech, requesting that caution be taken in anything anyone might be tempted to share publicly. This was out of respect for the Bardi-Jawi people, the Elders, and also out of respect for Mum. Frank Davey had appointed me as the public representative; anything put out publicly had to first be approved by me.

I guess we all slowly started to settle in with this new information. There was still so much to process. There will always be unanswered questions. One I was asked recently was, 'Do you think your Dad knew about your Mum's history?' I believe, he probably did know, but Dad could always be trusted to keep a confidence. He would have supported Mum's silence.

Some have also wondered why Mum's birth family took so long to make headway in their search. I remind them that there was no official record of Mum's birth. She had been given a new name, and the names, shown on her marriage record, were confusing. There is no mention of the name Quan Sing and her mother's name was almost impossible to read.

Mum had begun to disappear when she'd been given the name King and slipped even further away after making the choice to live as a white girl. And that's where it might have stayed. Then on 9 August this year, I was at another family gathering when the subject of Mum's story came up and someone had a few of the facts wrong.

That's when I decided, this story has to be written. Otherwise, what will happen, when I'm no longer around to set the record straight when someone gets it wrong? And by this time, I was becoming increasingly aware that Mum's story was part of a much, much bigger picture. The following day, I called my friend Cheryl.

Which brings me to the pointy end, where I have to try to put into words how this has affected me and how it's made me think and feel.

Right from primary school, I have not been able to help myself when it comes to defending the underdog. Looking back, I can see that I've been putting out spot fires all my life because I looked a bit different. Some people thought that I was a little bit Asian, some thought I was maybe Italian or Spanish.

This experience has only intensified my stance against racism and I feel far more strongly inclined to speak out about it now.

I guess I'd used humour to deflect attention, whenever any comments had been made in the past, good-natured for the most part, about the fact that I do look slightly Asian. About ten years ago, I started laughing along with it calling myself The Yellow Kid, whenever anyone had a friendly dig.

Since then, I've learned that The Yellow Kid was the name of a comic-strip character, in the US in the late nineteenth century. Around the time, the Quan Sing family was trading in Derby. Apparently, the comic strip explored themes like racial tension. I had no idea about this, I'd just made up the name. It was my way of laughing it off. But everyone has their limit. At some stage, we all reach a point, where we decide that enough's enough. Then we let rip.

Around the middle of this year, I was having drinks with a few girlfriends. We were talking about world events, as you do, and one of the girls said she recognised and deplored racism, but she didn't really get why people behaved that way. This was around the time when a lot was happening with the Black Lives Matter campaigns. I told her that it's hard to describe what it's like, until you experience discrimination, whether you're called out for your colour, looks or whatever. It comes in all forms, from the tiny little joke to full in your face. Although my friend does not have a racist bone in her body, I had to tell her that she probably couldn't really understand it because she was too white. There'd been no hiccups in her family, nothing anyone could latch on to, to have a dig. She'd never had to use humour to deflect attention away from herself, to turn a jibe into a bit of a joke. My friend's name is Karen. Then, the famous Bunnings Karen incident happened. This was where a woman, whose name was not Karen, had refused to wear a mask at a Melbourne Bunnings, during the Covid-19 restrictions and had been arrested by police. Dictionary.com defines the term Karen as slang for an obnoxious, angry, entitled and often racist middle-aged white woman.

The media labelled this woman a Karen and suddenly everyone had a Karen joke. They were all over Facebook, on the radio, in everyone's face. How did my friend Karen feel about this? 'I was laughing, too, at first,' she said.

'Some of the jokes were really funny. But when it went on, and on, and on, the humour started to wear thin. It wasn't funny any more. I was sick of it.'

'You can use that as an example of why people get sick and tired of being called names, when it happens all the time.'

This is just one of the reasons why I know this is not just my story. I happen to be the centrepiece here, but it is so much bigger than just the story of me, trying to find out who my Mum really was. There have been times, when this story has been like an old-fashioned ginger beer plant that just keeps on growing, flowing and moving. Now it's time to bottle it. And share it.

More than ever, I believe this story needs to be handed down, not just to Mum's descendants but to future generations, so they know what happened during that time in our history.

My niece Jessine has been particularly invested in this journey. She had taught in schools in remote Aboriginal communities, even before she'd learned that her grandmother had grown up as part of one. On my most recent trip back to visit Mum's country, Jessine came too. Before that trip, she had given me a card with a quote from Winston Churchill, 'Never, never, never give up'. Inside, she'd written a few words, thanking me for doing just that. The truth is that if I had given up, I might still be wondering.

As time ticked on, every so often I might still have found myself looking at Mum's photograph where she's wearing the green dress with her hair rolled back off her face. She looks so young in that photograph, so beautiful and so Chinese. If I hadn't stepped out, that day in 1981 and called on Julie's parents, armed with nothing more than a pen and my blue notebook, none of this might have happened.

16

THE MISSING YEARS

– JD & CR –

The missing years refers to different times in Marjorie's life, depending on who was searching. For Jennifer, the missing years were the first twenty-two years of Marjorie's life until she became engaged. That was when the first photographs of Marjorie had appeared and because there were no pictures of her parents or siblings, it had been easy to assume she had been an only child. This was a stark contrast to the York collection of family snaps that had increased as Marjorie and Henry's family grew.

Since events of May 2018, Jennifer has been able to fill many of the gaps and gain a good understanding of the people and early experiences that had helped shape her mother. Marjorie's passion for fishing, for example, is explained by her Sunday Island childhood and that connection with the ocean runs through her sons, daughters, grandchildren and great-grandchildren.

But to Marjorie's Bardi-Jawi family on the Dampier Peninsula, the time that she had shared with her York family were the years that were lost to them. After she'd been taken at thirteen to train and work at Derby Native Hospital, Marjorie had begun to fade out of their reach. Yet she never forgot her birth family. Every fortnight for years, she sent letters and parcels of treats, clothes and toys, home to her people on Sunday Island. There was never a return address. This contact had continued until Sunday Island Mission closed.

Jennifer believes Marjorie may have learned of the closure from one of her contacts, the missionaries on Sunday Island, where she sent letters and parcels or the Sharp sisters perhaps or even Mrs Ulrich through her network of contacts in the north-west.

Nothing has been found to indicate that Marjorie made contact with her birth family again after 1964, when the mission closed its doors. And by then, she had a husband and four young children.

17

TIMELINE OF EVENTS

Relevant to Marjorie D'antoine King York and the search that led to reunion

To save confusion in the following timeline, where the spelling Marjory was used in a source document, it has been corrected to Marjorie.

1899:

Sydney Hadleigh established a private mission on Sunday Island, at the entrance to King Sound in the Kimberley. From 1923 to 1929, the mission was run by the Australian Aborigines' Mission and by the United Aborigines' Mission from 1929 to 1934.[1]

1906:

The 1905 Aborigines Act came into effect in April 1906, creating the position of Chief Protector of Aborigines who became the legal guardian of every Aboriginal child in the State to the age of 16 years. The Act permitted authorities to 'send and detain' Aboriginal children in institutions and in 'service' (work).[2]

One of the Act's aims was to protect 'half caste' children fathered by settlers and who were not supported or educated by them. The legislation prevented mixed marriages and sexual relations between settlers and Aboriginal people. A policy of active assimilation was pursued, whereby 'half caste' children were removed from their families and placed in institutions to assimilate them into the European lifestyle.[3]

Around this time, the family of Quan Sing Yee Chun and Kimbly Ah Wing are established storekeepers in Derby. Their eleven Australian-born children were born in Derby, between 1896 and 1920.[4]

1915:

Auber Octavius Neville is appointed Chief Protector of Aborigines, a position he holds until 1936 when he becomes Commissioner For Native Affairs (CNA 1936-1940).[5]

1921:

Chief Protector of Aborigines A.O. Neville orders the cancellation of two permits that had been issued to eldest Quan Sing daughter, Yuanho (Una), to allow her to employ two Aboriginal workers. This was the latest episode in the battle between the Quan Sing family and the government, on the subject of Aboriginal employment.[6]

Another line of the Quan Sing family had already begun trading in Carnarvon. Son Lanky Quan Sing would later manage the waterfront store, after first working for his uncle.[7]

1924:

25 November Marjorie is born in Derby.[8,9]

(The Marjorie King Personal History Card erroneously shows her date of birth as June 1, 1926. This was a guesstimate. In 1944, as will be explained later in this timeline, the error was corrected, to November 25, 1924.)[8,9]

Marjorie's mother, Annie, of Sunday Island, was the daughter of a tribal marriage between Nundra, a full-blood woman, and pearler/

beachcomber Adrian Julius 'Frenchy' D'Antoine, formerly of The Seychelles. [10,11,12,13]

Marjorie's alleged father was described as The Quan Sing Man, Chinese, of Derby[9] and was believed to be Kinverns (Lanky) Quan Sing. Marjorie always said she knew this, and it is thought likely she had that information from Annie herself. [14]

It is believed Annie returned to Sunday Island, soon after Marjorie's birth, and it is there that Marjorie spent her childhood. Her early years were spent with her half-siblings, including her half-sister Maggie Ah Chu, who was four years older. Marjorie attended school in the morning, often looked after the younger children, and just loved to fish.[15]

1927:

9 March It is unlawful, under The Aborigines Act 1905 (WA), for unemployed Indigenous people to be in the City of Perth. The Perth Prohibited Area was enforced, from 1927 until it was abolished in 1954, requiring Aboriginal people to always carry a permit or Native Pass, if they wanted entry for any purpose, including work.[1,55]

1929-1939:

Australia is in the grip of the economic Great Depression, following the 1929 Wall Street stock market crash. By 1932, about 30 per cent of Australian workers are unemployed.[1]

1931:

22 May Adrien/Adrian Julius 'Frenchy' D'Antoine dies, Broome.[16]

25 November Marjorie is seven years old.

1932:

14 September Hubert Ulrich, 41, and Una Florence Austin, 33, marry in Queensland. He has worked as a pearler in Broome and Darwin, she as a nurse and midwife in remote regional Queensland.

They continue working in remote areas of Queensland, Hubert as a miner, until late in 1936, when they move to Western Australia. [17,18,19]

25 November Marjorie is eight years old.

1933:

25 November Marjorie is nine years old.

19 December *The Hobart Mercury*, Tasmania, runs a report of an interview with Mrs T. Street, of the United Aborigines' Mission, about activities on Sunday Island.

> The island…is very small, only about four miles long by three miles wide, and is the permanent home of some 120 native people…usually, the white population consists of three or four, there being two married couples doing the missionary work at present…The Mission runs a school for the children, and dormitories for those without parents or whose parents are away. Endeavours are made to make the parents responsible for their children as far as possible and to look after them in a proper manner. All of the children are given breakfast at the school, and the tiny ones are also provided with dinner, The bigger children fish a good deal, as there is any amount of fish around the island. At the school they receive instruction in writing, reading, arithmetic, and sewing, the girls making their own dresses. The natives are sometimes appointed as assistants.

The article reported Mrs Street as saying that the efforts of the male population were concentrated in gathering trochus shell, much of which was exported to England. Others worked in domestic service, as carpenters and there was a baker and butcher on the island. The women after leaving school were taught embroidery and crochet and gathered shells to make milk-jug covers and the like.

The report added that one of the greatest difficulties that missionaries had to face was the treatment by certain visiting pearlers, mainly Japanese, who practised immorality among the native girls.

> The utmost was done to combat this evil, but it was a difficult matter, and there was no way of effectively getting justice carried out in such an isolated place and under such conditions.
>
> Mrs Street said she could not say whether black-birding was carried on by the pearlers, as had been alleged recently, but she would not say it was not, as Sunday Island was further south than the territory concerned.[20]

(Black-birding, in this context, refers to the practice of kidnapping Aboriginal men and women, to work in the pearling industry, often as divers for pearl shell, and usually, for little or no reward.)

1934:

The Sunday Island mission and its people relocate to Wotjulum, near Yampi, before returning to Sunday Island in 1937.[1]

3 October Death of Mrs Kimbly Quan Sing, after a short illness.[21]

25 November Marjorie is 10 years old.

1936:

The Aborigines Act Amendment Act 1936 (or the Native Administration Act 1936) amended the 1905 Act and extended the power of authorities over Aboriginal people. The Chief Protector became the Commissioner for Native Affairs (CNA). The Commissioner was the legal guardian of all Aboriginal children to the age of 21, 'notwithstanding that the child has a parent'.

The Act also redefined the term 'native', to include all Aboriginal people, defined as being of 'full' descent, and any descendants 'of less than full blood', including 'half-caste' and also 'quadroons', who were under the age of 21, and who lived with other 'natives'. [22]

6 June Mr W.R. Holmes, of Gnowangerup, has been accepted on probation by the United Aborigines' Mission and appointed to Mount Margaret. Miss E. Doubikin has been appointed to Watjalum.[23]

13 June Perth Bible Institute farewells outgoing missionaries Mr Will Holmes and Miss Elsie Doubikin, St Andrews Church premises, Pier Street, Perth.[24]

25 November Marjorie is 12 years old.

1937:

1937 Electoral Roll lists William Robinson Holmes, Watjalum, via Derby, missionary.[25]

4 June After a short time, working at Moore River Native Settlement, Una and Hubert Ulrich are transferred north, to take up a one-year appointment, as nurse and officer-in charge, at Derby Native Hospital. They answer to A.O. Neville, former Chief Protector of Aborigines and now Commissioner for Native Affairs (CNA).[26]

17 June Mr Street writes in *The United Aborigines' Messenger*, telling how they have arrived at Derby to take up quarters there. Before leaving Watjulum, they had the joy of seeing Mr Holmes (presumably Will Holmes, see June 13, 1936) and Miss Doubikin united in matrimony.[27]

27 June Una F. Ulrich writes to the CNA, with unfavourable first impressions of Derby. She requests that the Department employ two 'half-caste' girls as she is unable to perform the double duty of nursing and cooking, over a hot stove, all through the wet season.[26]

25 November Marjorie is 13 years old.

1938:

9 January Marjorie is handed over by Mr Street of Sunday Island Mission to Mrs Ulrich of the Native Hospital, Derby, with the consent of the CNA, providing the local Protector concurred and the usual permit was taken out. Marjorie is to be trained by Mrs Ulrich and prior to the transfer, it is understood, Marjorie was running wild in the native camp at Sunday Island.[9]

7 March Mrs Ulrich reported that Marjorie wishes to attend school, which was arranged. Certain parents of white children objected to Marjorie attending the school, but no public protest was made, therefore Marjorie is still attending.[9]

31 May Annie and one of her younger children are admitted to Derby Native Hospital.[10]

28 June Personal History Card A311 is created for Marjorie King.[9] It states Marjorie was given the name of 'King' by CNA (A.O. Neville) after King Sound, whence Marjorie came. The card shows her age as 12 years, on 1 June 1938, but states that this date has been given to her by the CNA.

Parentage is shown as, Mother: H.C. 'Annie' of Sunday Island Mission. Alleged Father: Quan Sing, Chinese, of Derby. [9]

1 July Marjorie has now been taken away from school, on suggestion of CNA. She will be taught, in future, by a correspondence course from the Teachers' College, Claremont.[9]

18 August Una F. Ulrich again writes to the CNA, advising him 'The Faulkners brought Agnes here on the 8th of this month … Agnes … seems to have made things happier for Kate and Marjorie, who were not getting on very well and had had quite a fight a short time ago. However, they may be more peaceful with a third, than with just the two girls.

'I am giving…Marjorie…lessons daily, but will be glad when the correspondence lessons come for Marjorie…If Agnes is to be enrolled it would mean finding a surname for her and filling in another form.

'Can Kate use Kitchener as a surname. It would be better if she could have a surname. It may seem a small thing, but Marjorie has one and Kate who is older hasn't and it makes a little jealousy between them.' [26]

25 November Marjorie is 14 years old.

1939:

17 April Una F. Ulrich writes to the CNA, Perth, expressing discontent but stating: 'But I had the welfare of the natives and caste girls at heart and can do more than those who do not understand them; to improve their lot.'

Soon afterwards, the CNA and Mrs Ulrich meet to discuss her grievances.[26]

19 April A.O. Neville writes that he finds Mrs Ulrich is very sensitive to inference ... 'apparently she has taken notice of brief snatches of conversation not intended for her ears. However, I think she is happier about this matter now.'[26]

June The Ulrichs return to Derby, after a period of leave.[26]

3 September Prime Minister Robert Menzies announces that Australia is at war with Germany.[29]

October Marjorie obtains prizes at the (Perth) Royal Show for writing and fancy work.[9]

4 November Una F. Ulrich writes to CNA, A.O. Neville, advising that Marjorie has received second prize in her class for needlework, and Agnes Molloy third.

> Considering they competed with children from all over the State, I feel quite proud of them. Marjorie's writing was commended as also was Agnes' entry. Agnes has her illustrated story 'Very highly commended'. Agnes has done good work lately…Her teacher is keeping some of her work to use as

> specimen copies, to send to other pupils to show how the work should be done.
>
> This is very gratifying for the 'Supervisor' as you can well imagine. I want you to share in the pride of the work too, for they would never have had this chance if you had not made it all possible to them, first in sending them here and second in allowing them the correspondence lessons. I feel more than ever that 'training tells.' The Marjorie I received and the Marjorie of today are very different indeed. At first I doubted that I could do much to overcome her early lack of training, but now I am very much more satisfied. Agnes was younger and quieter natured, she too, is getting on well. [8]

24 November A.O. Neville replies, congratulating Mrs Ulrich and the girls.

> Considering the short time they have been with you, the results are astonishing and the examples of work, which I am returning to you to treasure, are outstanding…..
>
> When I was at the Settlement a few nights ago I enjoyed a social hour with the Staff and, to indicate my pleasure, I could not help telling them of the splendid results by Agnes and Marjorie. I did so to illustrate the possibilities in our children under proper tuition.[8]

25 November Marjorie is 15 years old.

1940:

20 March A.O. Neville writes to the Ulrichs, thanking them for cordial relations, on the eve of his long service leave and retirement. He thanks them for their excellent service.[26]

Neville's successor, as Commissioner for Native Affairs, was Francis Bray, who held the position from 1940 to 1946. [1]

July Una F. Ulrich resigns, without Hubert Ulrich's knowledge, but later, withdraws her notice. She is upset that help in the form of two girls from Moola Bulla, who she had been hoping to train as domestic servants, has not been forthcoming. They are not old enough.

In a letter to Acting CNA Francis Bray, she writes,

> .....Marjorie although a mere school girl has had to do this and has done very well indeed. However, I don't want to overwork her and also in the event of having any infant sent here from the Leprosaurium I felt an older girl would be necessary.

She adds: 'If I did leave I'd miss the children more than anything. I bring them up just as I would my own (if I had any) and we are really a little family in many ways.'[26]

27 July Marjorie has left school, and is helping in the hospital.[9]

29 August Hubert Ulrich also writes to Bray, advising that he has also written to Bishop Frewer,[30] asking for details of a prospective worker from Forrest River.

'Our own girls are at present too young......Marjorie even with the little training she has had is really an excellent girl, but is too young to be left on her own for any length of time.'[26]

(Anglican Bishop John Frewer was Bishop of the North-West of Australia from 1928 to 1965)[30]

29 September Rev. G.W. Holmes, of the Kunmunya Mission, pleas for the sympathetic understanding of the Australian aborigines, in a talk at St Andrews Presbyterian Church, in Perth.

Mr Holmes was reported to have said 'the continent was owned by its wild inhabitants until the British invaded the place and drove them into the far corners.

'In many cases their treatment by us was a stain on Australian history.'[31]

9 October Hubert Ulrich writes to the Acting CNA,

> Marjorie King, 14 1/2 our rising hope, stolid type but very bright in patches, remembers what she is told to do and does it well, can be trusted in everything, has the makings of a first-class cook and housekeeper generally. Is too young and is not forceful enough to take complete charge at present. Will make a good assistant in the theatre.[8] (This is not Marjorie's correct age. It is the age, as calculated from the 1 June 1926 birthdate, which had been estimated for her.)

16 November Una F. Ulrich writes to the CNA, Perth, asking that he consider putting Marjorie King on wages. 'She is doing a lot of work and doing it very well….'[26]

25 November Marjorie is 16 years old.

At some point in 1940, Una F. Ulrich gave Marjorie *The Golden Wattle Cookery Book*, in which she had written, 'For Marjorie in her 15th year, 1940, With every good wish for your future from Sister. U.F. Ulrich.' Beneath the signature is a smudge, recently identified as the word, Derby.[32]

1941:

6 March Marjorie is to be paid 5/- per week, 2/6d to Department (to hold in a Trust Account for her) and 2/6d to Marjorie.[9]

18 March The CNA writes to the Officer-in-Charge, Native Hospital, Derby,

> It has now been decided to allow Marjorie King wages to the extent of 5/-d per week as from the 1st February last. The amount to be paid to her is 2/6d per week as pocket money and the balance of 2/6d per week will be banked in this office on her behalf.

> The Treasury Paymaster is being advised to this effect and I shall be glad if you will kindly see that Marjorie collects her proportion of pocket money as from the arranged date.[8]

25 May Una F. Ulrich writes to the CNA, Perth, expressing fears for the girls if she leaves.

> Gwen is very attached to me and like Marjorie does not want me to leave her here if I do not return. When (Marjorie) came she couldn't and wouldn't do anything. Her main accomplishment was rushing to the front fence if anyone went by. The transformation of Marjorie alone would be a work to be proud of. Since she has been here she has learned to read and write, to mend and sew and do simple fancywork. She can wash and iron beautifully. She is an excellent plain cook, can cook meat and vegetables, puddings and pastry and cakes. She works neatly and cleanly and is generally careful. If anyone had told me three years ago I could train Marjorie into such a success I'd have laughed at them, I would not have believed it possible, but there it is.
>
> The only thing I put it down to is I have trained her in my own way and there has been no one to interrupt any of my methods or ideas, and had there been anyone else to pull down as fast as I built up, results would not have been so good.
>
> Marjorie's health has been consistently good and she is declared to be free of V.D.
>
> Marjorie's one anxiety is that she will be parted from me. She is very, very distressed at the idea of my not returning to Derby. [26]

15 July The new OIC at Derby Native Hospital, W.G. Trigg, writes to the CNA, asking for clarification, with regard to wages for Marjorie King.

> On our salary sheet I draw 5/- for her representing 2/6d per week pocket money. Is this all the wages she is paid or do you hold any balance on her account?
>
> If you hold any balance for her, what is the procedure when she wishes to purchase any clothes etc. Do I purchase them and charge up to the Native Affairs a/c Marjorie King or do I have to wait for a remittance from you to cover the cost of same?
>
> With regard to the other Half-Caste girls, I hold the balance of their wages in trust and out of it pay for anything they wish to purchase. Marjorie King cannot understand why she cannot do the same.

Would you please send me this information as soon as possible.[26]

23 July The CNA replies that,

> Marjorie is in receipt of 5/- per week, 2/6 of which you pay her as pocket money. The balance, 2/6 per week, is paid into her Trust account at this office and she is able to draw on the balance in that Trust account for any clothes (other than working) and extras that she may require. Working clothes will be supplied by the Department as she is on the wages of 5/- only.
>
> You are also required to submit, at the end of every six months, a report as to her capabilities and whether or not you consider her worthy of an increase of say 2/6 per week to be paid into the Trust account held here.
>
> Her bank balance here is now £3.13.8.[8]

In **September,** the CNA writes to Dr Haynes, in Derby, and W. G. Trigg, who with wife Ellen, has replaced the Ulrichs at the Derby

Native Hospital. Bray states that Mrs Ulrich is not to return to work. 'Her services have been dispensed with.'[26]

Bitter argument is evident, in correspondence from Una F. Ulrich to the Triggs and the CNA, later in the year. In October, Bray comments that he holds a high opinion of Mrs Ulrich, as a nurse, 'but I feel she was unsuited to the conditions at Derby.'[26]

1 October Una F. Ulrich writes an impassioned letter to the editor, *Daily News*, Perth, defending natives of the Kimberley.[33] This follows the publication of an article in which extremely racist language and attitudes are expressed.

26 October Marjorie writes from Native Hospital, Derby to CNA Bray, Native Affairs, Perth.

> Thank you ever so much for sending such nice shoes for us. It was very nice of you to do so. It might be interesting to you to know how we are getting on with our work. We are quite happy doing our duty and to help Mr and Mrs Trigg all we can. It is a nice home for us both to stay. We both have a lot of pleasure at home and sometimes we take little Wendy Ann for a little walk. Sometimes when (there is a) nice picture on they both take us with them. From Marjorie.[8]

19 November Una F. Ulrich writes to Marjorie, but the letter becomes the subject of a request from W.G. Trigg to Bray, asking that he write to Mrs Ulrich and either request, or order, her to cease writing to Marjorie King and Agnes Molloy.[26]

20 November The CNA replies to Marjorie King's October letter,

> I am pleased to hear from you, Marjorie, and to know that you like the shoes that were sent to you. I am glad that you enjoy your work and are doing your best to assist Mr and Mrs Trigg. I think that motion pictures are most interesting and educational

> and it is very kind of Mr Trigg to take you along occasionally. Continue to perform your duties well and I am sure you will always be a happy girl.[8]

25 November Marjorie is 17 years old.

30 November Rev. G.W. Holmes, of Kunmunya Mission, makes 'an earnest plea' for sympathetic treatment of the Australian aborigines, speaking at St Andrews Presbyterian Church, in Perth.

> There were various attitudes of mind towards the aboriginal, Mr Holmes said. Some said he was not human, and should be left alone. Others wanted to exploit his labour. Some regarded him as a 'museum piece' for investigation and research. Finally, there were those who believed that the aboriginal was made in the image of God and was capable of intellectual and spiritual development.[34]

9 December Bray responds to Mr W. Trigg saying that he considers the better course of action would be to intercept and suppress all correspondence 'to your inmates by virtue of your power under Regulation 39. If you take charge of all letters coming from Mrs Ulrich and watch also to see that no letters are written to her by your inmates, I think the matter would gradually subside.'[26]

1942:

3 March Japanese fighter planes bomb Broome.[35]While the death toll remains unknown, it is believed that at least 89 people died during the raid, including American, British, Dutch, Indian and Japanese military personnel and civilians.[38]

Marjorie's 23 year-old cousin, Charles D'Antoine, was refuelling a flying boat, containing Dutch refugees, in Roebuck Bay, when the fighter planes hit. He rescued a woman and child from drowning and was later presented with a certificate of merit from the Royal Humane

Society and four medals for bravery from the Royal Netherlands defence forces. But he received no recognition from the Australian military or government, because he was Aboriginal. WA author, the late Jan James, dedicated her 2011 book *Forever Warriors*, honouring indigenous men and women, who served in all conflicts, to Charles D'Antoine. [37,38,39]

10 March Marjorie is evacuated from Derby to Moola Bulla.[8]

20 March Japanese fighter planes bomb Broome and Derby.[40]

9 October CNA gives permission for Marjorie's and Agnes Molloy's return to Derby.[9]

19 October Marjorie and Agnes arrive in Derby. Marjorie's wages are 2/6d pocket money, 5/- payable to trust account.[9]

(According to the 1944 summary on the Marjorie King Personal File, she returned to Derby on 16 October 1942, when her wages were increased to 7/6d per week.)[8]

1943:

The Quan Sing family in Carnarvon, listed on the Australian electoral roll, are: Kinverns (storekeeper), Kingwell (producer), Kinton (driver), Winson (radio dealer), Yuanho (domestic), Lillian (home duties)[41]

25 November Marjorie is 19 years old.

1944:

5 September W.G. Trigg writes to the CNA, Perth,

> I enclose herewith an application from Marjorie King for a Certificate of Exemption from under the Native Act. Accompanying this application are references from Mr Watt and Mr Rowell. I also enclose a letter of recommendation from Dr Musso.
>
> Mrs Trigg and myself both think this girl is worthy of exemption. We have known this girl for over three years and can honestly

state that she has always conducted herself in a splendid manner and has always lived as a white girl.

Although Marjorie is employed as house girl at this hospital, all her time is occupied in our quarters and she does not have any contact whatsoever with the natives.

Marjorie is very keen to have the status of a white girl and I am of the opinion that she is worthy of it.[8]

5 September Marjorie King writes to the CNA,

I hereby wish to apply for a Certificate of Exemption from under the Native Act.

I am a quadroon girl and will be 20 years of age on the 25th of next November. At present I am a State ward employed by the Native Affairs Department as house girl to Mrs Trigg. Although I am employed at the Hospital, all my time is occupied in the Staff quarters and I do not have any contact whatsoever with any Native. I have always done my best to live as a white girl. I enclose herewith references from Mr Watt and Mr Rowell testifying to my living as a white girl.

I would very much like to have a Certificate of Exemption and would be very thankful if you would consent to same.[8]

6 September Hugh M. Watt, JP, writes,

I wish to state that I have known Marjorie King for thirteen years, and consider she is one worthy of exemption as she is an outstanding character.

She is a Christian with high ideals and has always been responsive to training and willing to accept helpful advice.

In my opinion, and from a public point of view, I think this girl worthy of all that can be done for her.[8]

6 September Dr Musso, Medical Inspector of Natives, Derby, writes,

> This is to testify that, since 1939, I have known a very light coloured quadroon girl called Marjorie King, aged 19 years, who has been staying at the Native Hospital, Derby, firstly, under the care of Mrs Ulrich and latterly under Mrs Trigg, except for a period during the evacuation emergency.
>
> From my observation of this girl at various times, I am of the opinion that she has been living, both morally and otherwise, up to standards well equal to the average white person. Although she is technically domiciled at a Native Institution, she is living and working in a part of the Staff quarters which is, naturally, up to high white standards and her social intercourse with any of the patients is practically nil. This is notwithstanding the fact that she is living with her half-caste friend, Agnes Molloy, who (i.e. Agnes) is likewise a fit candidate for exemption.
>
> On at least three occasions since 1939, the last of which was a few days ago, I have medically examined this girl finding no clinical signs of leprosy whatsoever.
>
> I have, therefore, no hesitation in recommending the application of this girl for exemption from the provisions of The Native Administration Act, provided she accompanies Mr and Mrs Trigg in the event of their transfer.[8]

18 September W.G. Trigg writes to the CNA, applying on behalf of Mrs Trigg and himself for the positions of Matron and Superintendent at the Carrolup Native Settlement,

> ... provided suitable arrangements could be made for Marjorie King to accompany us to be our house girl down there.

> Marjorie has been a very loyal and trustworthy servant to us during our three years here and Mrs Trigg has been responsible for her training. This girl has always led a good life, quite up to white standards, and we think she should be given a better chance in life and the opportunity to meet and mix with a better class of people.
>
> Marjorie has been very loyal and faithful and has never complained about her lot. She is only receiving 7/6d per week, whereas there are plenty of coloured girls not up to Marjorie's standard who are working in town and receiving between two pounds up to three pounds and ten shillings per week wages. There are plenty of white people in town who would be only too willing to employ Marjorie at a really good wage.
>
> I do not see why the leprosy question should bar Marjorie from going South. There are several coloured people who can travel about ad. lib. because they have an exemption or are granted permission….
>
> If you cannot arrange for Marjorie to accompany us as a State Ward, would you be prepared to allow Mrs Trigg to take out a guardianship of Marjorie until she attains the age of 21…
>
> The reason for Marjorie King applying for an exemption certificate was not in order to overcome the leprosy precautions in relation to her transfer South. Marjorie has always lived as a white girl and we really think she is worthy of an exemption. But if the exemption would debar her from coming to Carrolup with us then perhaps it might be advisable to hold it over for the time being…[8]

11 October Hon. Min. has refused Marjorie's application, for exemption from provisions of The Native Administration Act, as

Marjorie is recorded as a quadroon, therefore, she would not be a native, in law, owing to her high standard of living, if she resided elsewhere than the Native Hospital, Derby, where she is employed.[9]

The refusal is explained in full, in a letter from the CNA to the Hon. Minister for the North-West,

> Marjorie King, the first assistant at the Derby Native Hospital, has submitted an application for a Certificate of Exemption from the provisions of the Native Administration Act. Marjorie is eighteen years of age, and is recorded as a quadroon in our records, being the daughter of Annie, a half-caste, and allegedly her father was Quan Sing, of Derby.
>
> Marjorie's mother was possessed of Asiatic blood, and this means that although the girl is a quadroon according to our records, she possesses Asiatic blood on both sides of her parentage. She is a fairly well educated girl, and as an indication of this you will find her nicely written application at page 101, which is supported by the testimonials at pages 98, 99 and 100, and you will notice by the testimonial on the last-mentioned page that Dr Musso reports most favourably on Marjorie's behaviour and ability.
>
> However, there is a technical point involved in the matter. As Marjorie is a quadroon she would not be a native in law if she resided elsewhere than at the Native Hospital at Derby. This means in effect that she could easily obtain non-native status by leaving our employ at the Native Hospital. This is the legal position in the matter as it appears to me, and for this reason I consider that a Certificate of Exemption is unnecessary because Marjorie could easily secure non-native status by removing from the hospital....

> … Reverting to Marjorie King's application, she is ineligible at present since she is residing on a native reserve, and I recommend therefore that you do not approve of the application on this account. Our policy is against the retention of girls in our employment when they can receive better rates of remuneration at outside service, and this consideration should also be extended to Marjorie King, but since she is to be paid at the rate of £1 a week as from this date, I doubt whether she will now wish to leave the hospital, and feel that her application might be met if you refused it on the grounds that she is employed at the Native Hospital, which is a native reservation.[8]

(Marjorie is in fact six weeks away from her 20th birthday, given her birth date of 25 November 1924. Also, Annie's mother was Nundra, who was indigenous, and her father was Adrian Julius 'Frenchy' D'Antoine, a Frenchman from the Seychelles..[10,11,12,13])

Late 1944: A document, from the office of the CNA, on the Marjorie King file, summarises key points on the record, to date:

> Marjorie King appears as a quadroon in our records. Her mother, Annie (half-caste), daughter of Frenchy D'Antoine, white man, and a full-blood woman, lived at Derby for some years. Since 1939 Annie's name has been on the Sunday Island subsidy list. Allegedly, Marjorie's father is a Chinese named Quan Sing of Derby.
>
> Mr Neville gave her the surname of King in 1938, after King Sound, whence she came.
>
> Regarding her age, Marjorie's date of birth was unknown when she was transferred to the Derby Native Hospital and Mr Neville approved of Mrs Ulrich's suggestion that the date be recorded as the 1 June 1926 (now 18 years of age.) Later,

Mr Trigg ascertained from Mr Williams of the Sunday Island Mission that Marjorie was born on 25 November 1924 (now almost 20 years of age) and Marjorie, herself, has accepted the latter date as correct.

On 9 January 1938, Marjorie was handed over by Mr Street of the Sunday Island Mission to Mrs Ulrich, Matron of the Derby Native Hospital. This transfer was effected with the concurrence of the CNA and with the idea that Marjorie should receive training and at the same time be a companion to the native girl employed at the hospital

Mr Ulrich appeared to be a little dubious about accepting the responsibility of taking charge of Marjorie who, he stated, had been allowed to run wild in the full-blood camps at Sunday Island and would require careful handling for some considerable time. However, when transferred, Marjorie seemed very eager to learn and at her own request was enrolled at the Derby State School by Mrs Ulrich. To this some of the white parents objected, chiefly on the grounds that Marjorie had only recently come from a native camp. Although no official protest was lodged, at the suggestion of the CNA, Marjorie was quietly withdrawn from the school and arrangements were made for her tuition by Correspondence Course, under the guidance of Mrs Ulrich.

In October 1939, in competition with Correspondence pupils throughout the State, Marjorie received second prize in the (Perth) Royal Show for her needlework, and her handwriting was commended. In reporting this, Mrs Ulrich wrote: 'The Marjorie I received and the Marjorie of today are very different indeed. At first I doubted that I could do much to overcome her early lack of training but now I am very much more satisfied.

In June 1940, Marjorie was withdrawn from the Correspondence Classes after completing the work of Standard III, Mrs Ulrich being of the opinion that she had progressed as far as possible without undue strain. From the 1.2.41 Marjorie was placed on wages of 5/-d per week as a reward for her services at the Hospital.

On 25 April 1941, Mrs Ulrich reported that Marjorie was an excellent plain cook and that she could wash and iron beautifully, further, that if anyone had told her three years previously that she could train the girl into such a success she would not have believed it. This favourable opinion was not shared by Mrs Trigg when she first took over the Derby Native Hospital.

On the 12 September 1941 Mrs Trigg reported that Marjorie was not worthy of an increase in wages as she was far from satisfactory, Mrs Trigg attributing her shortcomings to bad training. At this time Marjorie was sharing a room with several Moola Bulla half-caste girls who worked in Derby during the day and returned to the Native Hospital at night

On 10 March 1942, Marjorie was evacuated to Moola Bulla. She returned to Derby on 16 October 1942 when her wages were increased to 7/6d per week. Marjorie is now employed in the staff quarters and Mr Trigg claims that she lives according to white standards and does not associate with natives.[8]

23 November Letter from the CNA to The acting Accountant, Chief Secretary's Department:

On the 5th October approval was given for the native girl Marjorie King, domestic at the Derby Native Hospital, to be paid at a weekly rate of £1 as from and including the 5 October 1944.

> At the time you were requested to arrange for a cash payment to Marjorie of 5/- per week and to credit her trust account at this Office with 15/- per week. Advice has now been received from the Officer-in-Charge of the Derby Native Hospital that the proportion to be paid in cash to Marjorie should be 10/- per week. Will you therefore please arrange as from and inclusive of 24 November 1944, the payment at Derby to Marjorie King in cash 10/- per week and credit 10/- per week to her trust account at Head Office. Will you please also instruct the Treasury Paymaster at Derby to this effect.[8]

25 November Marjorie is 20 years old.

1945:

Early in 1945, the Rev. Mr G.W. Holmes writes to the Acting CNA, requesting to secure the services of Marjorie King.

In **mid-February,** the Acting CNA replies to Mr G.W. Holmes, PO Box 3, Post Office, Broome, approving the request:

> ....I have discussed your request with the Hon. Minister for the North-West, and he feels that your proposal would certainly be advantageous to Marjorie, especially as you are removing altogether from the Kimberleys to more settled areas.
>
> Marjorie has given excellent service at the Derby Native Hospital over a period of years, and in addition she has been receiving training from two exceptionally well-qualified Matrons, and therefore I feel certain that she will do well and be of good behaviour wherever she may be employed and reside.
>
> I am forwarding a copy of this communique to Mr Trigg, and it will be necessary for you to contact him and make all the necessary arrangements for Marjorie's transfer from Derby to Broome. These expenses must be borne by yourself.

> Would you please arrange to submit periodical reports respecting Marjorie, say each six months, in order that I may be satisfied that she is well and happy. I feel that you should also arrange for her medical examination each six months in order that she may be declared free from any signs of leprosy infection. These medical examinations should be continued for at least five years, and the medical certificates forwarded to this Department for record purposes.
> When Marjorie King ceases employment at the Derby Native Hospital, and providing she does not further associate with natives, she will not be regarded as a native in law.[8]

19 February The Acting CNA writes to the Hon. Minister for the North-West:

> I should be pleased if you would kindly note the action I have taken in respect to the quadroon girl, Marjorie King. I have approved of her transfer to Broome for employment with Mr and Mrs Holmes, the former being the late superintendent of Kunmunya Mission. If you remember this decision was made in consultation with your good self … [8]

25 February Marjorie King writes to the CNA:

> Thank you ever so much indeed for giving me the opportunity to go to Carnarvon to work for Mr Holmes. I am very happy to leave Derby. I will do all I can to help them. I'm sure I'll be very happy. I know they are very nice people. Thanking you very much indeed for all you have done for me. Wishing you all the best of everything. Yours faithfully. Marjorie King.[8]

Early in 1945, Rev. George Holmes, formerly of Kunmunya Mission, has accepted a role as supervisor at the Australian Inland Mission Welfare Centre, in Carnarvon.[42,43]

March Claims by West Kimberley Road Board chairman H.M. Watt, J.P. that Marjorie King is unhappy at the thought of leaving Derby Native Hospital and is reluctant to proceed to Carnarvon with Mr and Mrs Holmes are investigated and considered to be unfounded.[8]

On **15 March,** the Acting CNA writes to Mr L. O'Neill, Inspector of Natives, Broome, concluding:

> When you visit Carnarvon it is my desire that you interview Marjorie King and satisfy yourself that she is happy and contented with Mr and Mrs Holmes. If you find that she is not, then I will arrange for action to be taken to effect her transfer elsewhere. [8]

19 April Ellen Trigg, now based with her husband and child, at Carrolup Native Settlement, via Katanning, writes to Acting CNA C.L McBeath:

> After all the bother over Marjorie King before our departure from Derby – I thought perhaps you may be interested to read the first letter I have received from her. I am enclosing same.

An extract from that enclosed letter to Mrs Trigg from Marjorie reads:

> … I have to look after their children. Mothers were very pleasant. I am getting 15 shillings a week and save it all, sheets and other things Mrs Holmes gets for me. I haven't been around the town yet but some day Mrs Holmes and I will take a walk and look at the places. They have lovely flowers growing here and houses are nice looking too. The house in which we live is quite a big place, every floor has to be polished, they are easy to do big rooms. I've got a lovely big room, polish it

> every week. I have found (it) very hard trying to do cooking with fat, they only give a little butter for our meals, we have plenty of meat which is not rationed, 1 pint of milk a day. I haven't been to the pictures yet, I went to a place last week but we had some people for supper so they made us stop home. Mr Holmes's mother is coming next week to stay here for holiday. I'll never see Derby again and all the people and the Watts, after seeing life here they'll never get me back, not for anything in the world. I like here and (am) happy and settling down, everything is like home to me, never for one minute do I think of Derby and not home sick at all, every morning is always lovely, nice weather, cool nights, a lot to see. Well, I better close now. I hope I'll see you again, thanking you very much for all you have done for me. Kind regards to Boss. Love to Wendy. Lot for yourself, from Marjorie.[8]

2 May The Deputy Commissioner of Native Affairs replies to Ellen Trigg's letter, thanking her and adding:

> Marjorie appears to be quite happy in her new surroundings and has settled in well with Mr and Mrs Holmes. I am very pleased to hear this, especially as I still propose that Inspector O'Neill should interview Marjorie when he visits Carnarvon later on in the year. [8]

8 May Celebrations begin to mark the end of World War II in Europe, known as Victory Europe or VE Day.[29]

9 May Rev. Holmes gives an address at the official VE Day celebrations in Carnarvon.[44]

10 August The CNA writes to Miss Marjorie King, c/- Mr G.W. Holmes, AIM Centre, Carnarvon:

> Dear Madam, I have to advise you that you have a credit of

> £18.18.6 in a Trust Account in your name at this office. In view of the fact that you do not now come under the jurisdiction of the Native Administration Act, you are entitled to control your own finances.
>
> If you desire, a cheque for the total balance of your credit, will be forwarded to you and I would be glad to hear from you in this regard.
>
> I trust you have fully settled down in your new position and are happy with Mr and Mrs Holmes.[8]

15 August VP (Victory in the Pacific), or VJ (Victory over Japan) Day celebrations begin to mark the end of World War II.[29]

25 November Marjorie is 21 years old.

1946:

1 March The Rev. Holmes, Presbyterian Minister at Carnarvon, for the past 12 months, recently left Carnarvon to take up residence in Perth, so as to enable him to continue his studies, with a view to taking up missionary work amongst the Australian Aborigines. [45,46]

10 May Marjorie King writes to CNA Bray from Lawley Ladies' College, 35 Glenroyd Street, Mt Lawley. This is the college and hostel run by sisters Rosalie and Mabel Sharp.

> Please kindly forward credit of £18.18.6 that you have in my trust account in your Office as it will come in handy for my training. You will see by my new address that I have left Carnarvon and have a new position and am very happy. I have taken dress making and enjoy it very much. I must thank you again for giving me my freedom. Mr and Mrs Holmes are here in Perth, they like it very much. I like being here, it is a lovely place and lot to learn. I am hoping to take music lessons very soon and other useful training.[8]

Marjorie remained in contact with the Sharp sisters into the 1960s, when they would drive out to visit her at West Swan. Jennifer remembers them, and their 'big, flash car.'

That training led to Marjorie finding employment as a nursing aide at Mount Hospital in Perth, and soon afterwards, she met Henry York.

1947:

9 September The engagement is announced between Miss Marjorie King and Mr Henry Stephen York, fourth son of Mrs and the late Mr G. W. York, of West Swan.[47]

1948:

10 April Marjorie D'Antoine King and Henry Stephen York marry at St Andrews Presbyterian Church in Perth and start life together on a small farm in West Swan.

(The name D'Antoine appears as Dantau/Dantan on the original marriage certificate; it was 2018 before the correct spelling D'Antoine was revealed).

1949:

April Marjorie and Henry York's son Philip is born. Before the delivery, Una F. Ulrich and Henry York argue, and the rift between them remains until Dawn York's wedding reception in 1975.[48]

1951:

18 May Kinverns (Lanky) Quan Sing wins a seat on Carnarvon Municipal Council, polling 103 votes to his rival's 36 votes.[49]

1953:

February Marjorie and Henry York's daughter Dawn is born.

27 August Kinverns (Lanky) Quan Sing dies suddenly in Perth[7,50]

1954:

June Marjorie and Henry York's son George is born.

1955:

From **1955**, the Caversham racing circuit west of the York farm is the venue for the annual Six Hour Le Mans end race until 1968.[51]

1957:

4 March Caversham circuit is venue for the Australian Grand Prix, and again, on 18 November1962.[52]

October Marjorie and Henry York's daughter, Jennifer, is born.

Annie D'Antoine's mother, Nundra dies, Sunday Island.[53]

1960:

19 February Annie D'Antoine dies on Sunday Island.[12]

1961, 1962, 1963:

Swan Districts Football Club win three back-to-back premierships.[54]

It is around this time, that Jennifer becomes aware there are gaps in her mother's history. Her father's family are regular visitors to their West Swan home, but where are her mother's family?

1964:

1 July The Aborigines Act 1905 was repealed, along with all subsequent amendments to the 1905 Act, by the Native Welfare Act 1963, which came into effect on 1 July 1964. The Commissioner of Native Welfare was no longer the guardian of Aboriginal children, but was responsible for the 'custody, maintenance and education of the children of natives.'[1]

1972:

1 July The Aboriginal Affairs Planning Authority Act 1972 commenced on 1 July 1972, repealing the Native Welfare Act 1963. The Act was designed to provide consultative and other services for the economic, social and cultural advancement of persons of Aboriginal descent in Western Australia. The Act abolished the Department of Native Welfare and created the Aboriginal Affairs Planning Authority.[1]

1975:

25 May Marjorie and Henry York's elder daughter, Dawn, marries Jim Bonzas. Una F. Ulrich travels from Queensland to attend the wedding. At the wedding reception, the rift between Mrs Ulrich and Henry York is settled.

When Mrs Ulrich is about to return to Queensland, she presents Jennifer with a copy of The Bible as a thank-you gift. She has written an inscription inside. It will be forty-five years before the inscription is interpreted as 'We are all equal.'

1981:

Late 1981 Jennifer begins interviewing members of the Quan Sing family and others with knowledge of Carnarvon history. No-one has ever heard of Marjorie King.

Aboriginal family history records:

From the period from **1921 to 1972**, the Native Welfare Department and its predecessor departments compiled a collection of personal files with information about Aboriginal people and their families. In **1972**, approximately 17,000 of these personal files were moved from State archives to the Department of Community Welfare, later the Department of Child Protection, to provide information about the adoption of Aboriginal children.

In **2017**, more than 16,000 of these personal files were transferred to the Aboriginal History Research Services, which is part of the Department of Local Government, Sport and Cultural Industries at the State Library of Western Australia.[56]

EPILOGUE

– JD –

One of my recurring questions as a child was, 'Where are the photographs of Mum, before she met Dad?' In 2018, when I took Mum back to country, the Davey family presented me with a family photograph showing Mum at about the age of six. The age I had been when I first began questioning Mum's past. It was the first photograph I had ever seen of Mum as a child and although I did not recognise that little girl, I did notice similarities with my sister, some of my nieces and even a glimpse of me.

The following year, Dawn, Jim, Geoff and I returned to visit Mum's grave and install a plaque we'd had made. It reads,

MARJORIE D'ANTOINE KING YORK

25.11.1924 – 9.07.2007

Loving wife to Henry Stephen York, devoted mother
of Philip, Dawn, George and Jennifer, caring
grandmother and great-grandmother.

'Our saltwater girl'

In 2020, I made my third visit to the Davey family and Ardyaloon, on the Dampier Peninsula, Mum knew as a child and which is now her final resting place. This time, my niece Jessine was with me.

Back in Broome on that trip, we made our first visit to the Sisters of St John of God (SSJG) Heritage Centre archives. It had been recommended to us by Glenis Ayling as an amazing collection and we were hoping to find photographs of Mum and information about Derby Native Hospital. Although we were not successful finding them on that visit, I was absolutely delighted to find a photograph of Mum's mother Annie, my grandmother. She is dressed up in her Sunday best and from the expression on her face, I can tell what a gentle person she was. It is also obvious that like Mum she had a fun-loving side too.

Jess and I returned to the Kimberley in July 2021 and made our second visit to the SSJG Heritage Centre. Jess took off and jumped straight on to the computer to search the catalogue, while I made my way to the information desk. I was talking to support officer Sarah Keenan when Jess suddenly called out, 'I think I've found a photo of Grandma!'

There was an image of a group of people up on screen. As the cursor hovered over each person in the image that person's name would appear. And there was Mum! I couldn't believe it, we hadn't seen anything like this on our previous visit.

It is impossible to adequately explain here, just how excited I felt in that moment. In fact, there were four photographs of Mum with others including Mrs Una F. Ulrich. One of the photographs was taken after a fishing trip.

Later, I learned that these images had been amongst a collection of photographs, donated some six years earlier by the Austin family from Queensland. The Austins were related to Mrs Ulrich. A condition of donation was that they be for personal use only and I agree with that. They are very personal to me as they are of my Mum and I will not be sharing them here.

I have learned that the photographs were uploaded on to the SSJG database on 3 April 2018, the month before that email from James Feehan had found me, thanks to the Quan Sing connection. The likely reason why I had not seen these photographs on an earlier visit was that the process of cataloguing, archiving, scanning, enhancing and uploading images requires a huge commitment and takes time to do properly. Then there is the process of entering names, dates and locations, where known. In circumstances where no annotation accompanies the photographs, the centre relies on information provided by volunteers with local and historical knowledge.

I do not know the Austin family and may never meet them, but will forever be grateful that they bothered to find a home for a bundle of photographs that might otherwise have been ignored or discarded and then would have been lost to me. This discovery has filled such a big void in the information that I had about Mum's early life. I am overjoyed to now have photographs of Mum as a young child, a teenager and as a young woman.

Hopefully, this may encourage anyone reading this to donate to public archives old photographs and information that may be of relevance to others. You may end up passing on a gift of immeasurable value to someone unknown to you, as the Austin family's donation did for me.

ENDNOTES

1 More about Sunday Island History, Government Departments and State Government Acts affecting Aboriginal people, and The Great Depression can be found on the Find and Connect website: https://www.findandconnect.gov.au/guide/wa;

2 Aborigines Act (1905): https://aiatsis.gov.au/sites/default/files/catalogue_resources/52790.pdf;

3 Assimilation Policy in Aborigines Act (1905): https://aiatsis.gov.au/sites/default/files/catalogue_resources/52790.pdf;

4 Quan Sing Family History Research by Glenis Ayling, personal. comm.;

5 Auber Octavius Neville, Australian Dictionary of Biography http://adb.anu.edu.au/biography/neville-auber-octavius-7821;

6 Yuanho (Una) Quan Sing's battle with the authorities is described here:

'The privilege of employing natives: The Quan Sing affair and Chinese Aboriginal employment in Western Australia, 1889–1934' by Victoria Haskins. https://ogma.newcastle.edu.au/vital/access/manager/Repository/uon:10723;

7 Popular Carnarvon Businessman Passes On, a report on the life and death of Kinverns (Lanky) Quan Sing: Northern Times (Carnarvon, WA : 1952–1954), Thursday 3 September 1953, page 1.

http://nla.gov.au/nla.news-article253688892;

8 Private Family History Record managed and researched by the Aboriginal History Research Services (AHRS) at the Department of Local Government, Sport and Cultural Industries (DLGSC): Native Welfare Personal Files, Department of Native Affairs, Quadroon – Marjorie King – of Sunday Island Mission – Personal File, Cons 1351, 1937/0855;

9 Private Family History Record managed and researched by the AHRS at the DLGSC: Personal History Card – Marjorie King, Cons 7105, A311;

10 Private Family History Record managed and researched by AHRS at the DLGSC: Annie Ah Chu, Cons 7105, Card A 664;

11 Aboriginal Shipbuilding Oral History – Doug D'Antoine, Derby, http://museum.wa.gov.au/research/collections/interviews/maritime-history-oral-histories/aboriginal-shipbuilding-oral-history);

12 Private Family History Record managed and researched by the AHRS at the DLGSC: Native Welfare Personal Files, Department of Native Affairs, Annie D'Antoine, Cons 1351, 1957/0357;

13 Private Family History Record managed and researched by the AHRS at the DLGSC Native Welfare Personal Files, Department of Native Affairs, Annie D'Antoine, Nundra, Sunday Island Mission – Register of Inmates, Cons 1351, 1950/0367;

14 Comment about Kinverns (Lanky) Quan Sing: Pers. comm. Jennifer Durrant;

15 Comments about Marjorie's early years and lifestyle on Sunday Island: Pers. comm. Jennifer Durrant in conversation with Frank Davey, Dorothy Hunter and the late Margaret Davey;

16 Announcement of 'Frenchy' D'Antoine's death: The West Australian (Perth, WA: 1879–1954), Weds 27 May, 1931, page 13;

17 Una Austin and Hubert Ulrich wedding report: Northern Standard. Darwin, Tuesday, October 18, 1932, p.3, .http://nla.gov.au/nla.news-article48043968;

18 Una Florence Austin born April 24, 1899, Queensland: Australian Birth Index 1788–1922;

19 Staff file held by State Records Office, Perth: Item 1937/0071 v 1 – Ulrich, Mrs and Mrs H. (Officer-in-charge and Nurse, Hospital, Moore River Native Settlement) and v2 – (Officer in Charge and Nurse, Derby Native Hospital);

20 Report on Sunday Island, in interview by Beryl Street, 1933: Mercury (Hobart, Tas.1860–1954), Tuesday 19 December 1933, page 12;

21 Death of Mrs Kimbly Quan Sing: West Australian (Perth, WA : 1879–1954), Monday 15 October 1934, page 10;

22 Extension of power of authorities over Aboriginal people: Native Administration Act 1936 https://nla.gov.au/tarkine/nla.obj-55208730;

23 Mission work by Mr W.R. Homes and Miss E. Doubikin: The West Australian, Saturday 6 June, 1936, page 23;

24 Farewell for outgoing missionaries Will Holmes and Elsie Doubikin: The West Australian, Saturday 13 June, 1936, page 25;

25 Missionary William Robinson Holmes is at Watjulum, via Derby: Australian Electoral Rolls 1903–1980;

26 Staff file held by State Records Office, Perth: Item 1937/0071 v 2 – Ulrich, Mr and Mrs H. (Officer-in-charge and Nurse, Derby Native Hospital);

27 William Robinson Holmes/Elsie Doubikin wedding reported: The United Aborigines' Messenger, Vol 5., No. 6, June, 1937;

28 Jennifer's thoughts on her mother's eye injury. Pers. comm. Jennifer Durrant;

29 Significant dates in World War II from DVA (Department of Veterans' Affairs) (2020), Australia and the Second World War, DVA Anzac Portal, accessed 30 December 2020, and Victory (8 May 1945/15 August 1945), accessed 31 December 2020, http://anzacportal.dva.gov.au/wars-and-missions/world-war-ii-1939–1945;

30 Australian Dictionary of Biography, Frewer, John (1883–1974) by Peter Boyce, http://adb.anu.edu.au/biography/frewer-john-10251;

31 Rev. G.W. Holmes, of Kunmunya Mission, pleas for sympathetic understanding of Australian Aborigines: West Australian (Perth, WA : 1879–1954), Tuesday 1 October 1940, page 5;

32 Inscription inside front cover of Golden Wattle Cook Book, given to Marjorie King by Una, F. Ulrich, now in possession of Jennifer Durrant;

33 Una F. Ulrich's letter to the editor, Daily News (Perth, WA : 1882–1950), Wednesday 1 October 1941, page 5;

34 Rev. G.W. Holmes, of Kunmunya Mission, talks about treatment of Aborigines: West Australian (Perth, WA:1879–1954), Tuesday, 2 December, 1941, page 6;

35 Japanese fighter planes bomb Broome: West Australian (Perth, WA : 1879–1954), Wednesday 4 March 1942, page 5;

36 Casualties and heroism noted with regard to Broome bombing: Broome Historical Society and Museum https://broomemuseum.org.au;

37 Book dedicated to Charles D'Antoine, who rescued a woman and child from the waters of Roebuck Bay during the bombing raid: Forever warriors : this book honours all Western Australian Indigenous men & women who served in all conflicts / Jan (Kabarli) James (2011), ISBN 9780959413526;

38 Story about Charles D'Antoine: The West Australian, March 1, 2011, War hero waits for honour, by Flip Prior: https://thewest.com.au/news/wa/war-hero-waits-for-honour-ng-ya-178968;

39 Interview with Charles D'Antoine's sister, Peggy Clements, with Vanessa Mills, ABC radio, March 2, 2012: https://www.abc.net.au/local/audio/2012/03/02/3444483.htm;

40 Derby and Broome bombed: West Australian (Perth, WA : 1879–1954), Monday 23 March 1942, page 5;

41 Quan Sing family on voter list in Carnarvon, 1945: Australian Electoral Rolls 1903-1980;

42 Awaiting arrival of Rev. G.W. Holmes in Carnarvon: Northern Times (Carnarvon, WA : 1905–1952), Presbyterian Church Notes, Friday 2 March 1945;

43 Rev. George Holmes to replace Rev. Dawson in Carnarvon: Northern Times (Carnarvon, WA : 1905–1952), Presbyterian Church Notes, Friday 19 January 1945, page 3;

44 Rev. Holmes gives address at V-E Day celebrations, Carnarvon: Northern Times (Carnarvon, WA: 1905-1952), Friday 11 May, 1945, page 2;

45 Rev. Holmes has left Carnarvon for Perth. Northern Times (Carnarvon, WA: 1905–1952), Friday, 1 March 1946, page 14;

46 Carnarvon awaits a successor to the Rev. G. Holmes at the Australian Inland Mission (Presbyterian): Northern Times (Carnarvon, WA: 1905–1952), Friday, 8 March, 1946, page 15;

47 Announcement of the engagement of Marjorie King and Henry Stephen York: The West Australian (Perth, WA:1879-1954), Tuesday, 9 September 1947, page 14;

48 Events at the birth of her brother, Philip York, in 1949: Pers. comm. Jennifer Durrant;

49 Kinverns (Lanky) Quan Sing is elected to council: The West Australian (Perth, WA: 1879–1954), Friday 18 May 1951, page 9;

50 Kinverns (Lanky) Quan Sing dies suddenly in Perth: The West Australian (Perth, WA: 1879–1954), Friday 28 August 1953, page 12 http://nla.gov.au/nla.news-article49229172

51 Le Mans car racing at Caversham: https://wannerooraceway.com.au/6-hour-le-mans-1968-to-1972/;

52 Grand Prix races at Caversham: http://www.australiaforeveryone.com.au/files/perth/caversham.html;

53 Death of Nundra: Births, Deaths and Marriages, Death in the State of Western Australia. 1882–1957;

54 Swan Districts Football Club premiership history: https://www.swandistrictsfc.com.au/the-club/history;

55 Perth's prohibited area: https://culture.wa.gov.au/feature/perths-prohibited-area#block-mainnavigation;

56 Information about family history records that are managed and researched by the Aboriginal History Research Services (AHRS) with the Department of Local Government, Spot and Cultural Industries (DLGSC): Letter to Jennifer Durrant from Melanie Walley-Stack, Director, Aboriginal Culture and History (WA), June 5, 2018.

ACKNOWLEDGEMENTS

Many willing hands helped Jennifer resolve the mystery of her mother Marjorie's past and led to this story of her search being published.

Thank you Diane Evans and the team at Big Sky Publishing for recognizing the significance of the story and for all your support, encouragement and professionalism in seeing this book take shape.

There are those who never gave up, notably the Davey family, who have so warmly welcomed Jennifer into their lives. James Feehan and the Kimberley Stolen Generation Aboriginal Corporation facilitated that reunion, by taking a new approach to a cold case when the chance of success seemed remote. Without your persistence, we might all still be wondering.

Special thanks to Julie QuanSing-Rowlands, Glenis Ayling and the extended Quan Sing family for their willingness to help and share what they knew of their family history. Your generosity helped form the bridge between Marjorie's birth family and Jennifer.

Marilyn Horner and her extended family including Verna and Bill Campbell, deserve mention for Marilyn's independent research, and for asking the questions that led to Jennifer's eventual connection with her Quan Sing cousins.

Thank you to all the staff and volunteers at The Sisters of St John of God Heritage Centre, Broome, for keeping records for people like Jennifer to access when they come looking. In particular, archivist

Helen Mary Martin and support officer Sarah Keenan, your time and commitment is greatly appreciated. You went above and beyond in helping Jennifer access for personal use the photographs of Marjorie as a teenager, and also her grandmother, Annie. The archive is funded entirely by the Sisters of St John of God, with some private funding. The Centre receives no government help. The Ulrich family descendants' donation of their photographic collection, not knowing that it contained photographs Jennifer had been longing for, proved to be a remarkable gift.

Online resources including the National Library of Australia's newspaper archive, Trove, and ancestry.com.au were invaluable in fleshing out the back stories to key players in Marjorie's life, including Mabel Ross Sharp and her sister Rosalie Ross Sharp, Hubert and Una F. Ulrich, William Robinson Holmes and the Rev. George Holmes.

Others who helped this story on its journey include Claudine, Mitch, Gavin and the team at Bankwest, Perth; Munya Andrews, Christine_p47, Jan Pond, Anne Cook, Marilyn Carson, Marilyn 'Maz' Rogers, Alan Patton, Ron Carey, Beverley Cottrell, Geoff D'Cruz, Errol Barrett, Maria Weighell, Leanne Old, Lisa Miles and Allison Heinritz. Former Caversham teachers Les Butcher and the late Alan C. Lindsay deserve thanks for instilling the skill of speed reading and the value of never, ever giving up when running a race.

Last but not least, thanks Heather Zubek for the gift that led us to the Big Sky Publishing team in the first place.

ABOUT THE AUTHORS

Jennifer Durrant worked in Finance for 44 years, and spent much of her life wondering where her mother Marjorie came from. She loves swimming in the ocean, cycling, communing with nature, and enjoys long lunches with friends. She volunteers for her coastal community, working with wildlife, senior Australians and her local MP.

Former journalist Cheryl Rogers writes around the edges of farming and family life in the Swan Valley, near Perth. Her short fiction has been published in Australia, the UK and USA, and she is a three time winner of the Henry Lawson Society of New South Wales short story award and previously had a co-written memoir short-listed for the WA Premier's Book of the Year Award. A long-time member of Sisters in Crime (Australia), Cheryl loves a mystery.